One Egg Noodles

Recipes That Hold Us Together

By Shannyn Cook Caldwell, T.N.D.

An Imprint of
Heavens to Betsy Press
Las Cruces, NM 88001
© 2025 The Healing Season, LLC.

This publication contains the opinions and ideas of its author. It is intended to provide helpful information on the subjects addressed in this publication. It is sold with the understanding that the author and publisher are not engaged in rendering medical, health, or other personal professional services. The reader should consult their medical, health, or other competent professional before adopting any of the suggestions in this book or drawing inferences from it.

The author and publisher disclaim all responsibility for any liability, loss, or risk, personal or otherwise, that is incurred consequently, directly or indirectly, of the use and application of any of the contents of this book.

All rights reserved, including the right to reproduce this book or portions thereof in any form whatsoever.

Heavens to Betsy Press: Celebrating 15 years in publishing.

You can invite Shannyn Caldwell to speak at your event. For information, visit our website, www.shannyncaldwell.com.

Made In the United States of America
ISBN: 979-8-9927893-1-7
Imprint: Heavens to Betsy Press 2025
All Bible references taken from the NASB

I have been young and now I am old,

Yet I have not seen the righteous forsaken

Or his descendants begging for bread.

Psalm 37:25

Acknowledgments

To the team of Heavens to Betsy Press-

To my daughter and editor, Alexandra Biedenbach: Thank you for the inspiration and dedication. I am so proud of you. Thanks for believing in this project and this mama.

I'm so glad you loved the noodles on that day.

To my son, Liam: Thank you for the laughter, insight, and the boldness with which you pursue your vision and for your inspired illustrations.

To Stephen Austin: Thank you for the gorgeous final edit.

To the team at 7 Sound: You really are a dream team and you've made this process blessed bliss.

To Heather Cohen from Small House for the push.

Thanks to my radio coach and friend Beth Bacall, who said the words "One Egg Noodles" in a way that hung in the air and stuck.

To the Family Life Radio and Intentional Life Media team, thank you.

Thank you to the people along the way who have been generous with their meals and recipes.

And thank you, Jesus, who reminded me one day that even though the grocery prices were wrecking my budget, to give Him what I have. He still does His thing with loaves, fishes, and sometimes your very last egg.

Excerpted from my book *The Healing Season: How a Deadly Tornado Wrecked and Reshaped My Faith*

I cried out to the Lord in my heart because I did not have one dollar to feed my family, not one buck to go to the dollar store and get some noodles. We were broke. Along with most of our foreclosed-on neighbors, we were teetering on the edge of the cliff of bankrupting Detroit.

Then, the tender voice of our loving Father spoke to me again. "I know your heart, little mother."

I felt so known and understood because I didn't want the food for me. I could fast. I wanted food for them. For my kids, and I thought, how could this be? I've got an education. I've got experience. We live a simple life. Why can't I feed my kids? Why can't my husband?

And just then, the Lord gave me a picture of a giant bowl full of flour. There was a pit in the center of the flour and then I saw an egg crack over the bowl and land in the pit. Then a spoon full of water poured in and began to stir. This, I thought, is how my grandma Kay used to make homemade pasta growing up! I remembered it now.

I went to the kitchen. Checking in my fridge, I found one egg, flour, a little bit of butter and the bottom of a shaker of parmesan. I followed the recipe the Lord provided and made homemade noodles for dinner that night. The kids still swear it's the best meal I've ever made, and they do not know that we were broke the day I first made it.

For years they asked for my homemade noodles. For years I kept the origan secret-not wanting to pass on the idea of poverty and lack to the next generation.

Then one day I spilled it, and they loved them even more.

Almost 20 years later, with so much more stability, my kids and I have been so blessed to try noodles of all kinds. We even got to taste noodles in London and Paris recently. On the last day of our most recent trip to London, we had dinner at an Indian restaurant I had wanted to visit for years. We sipped on Jasmine tea and felt relaxation steep our bones and inspiration season our minds. "Wow, Mom," Alex said. "We sure have come a long way since "one-egg noodles."

I pray this book blesses you and your family wherever you find yourself on the path of life. I hope it fills your heart with hope and your belly with bliss.

Contents

    Preface

    Part One: The Healing Kitchen

1. Things that Bind Us

    Eggs & Gluten Free Binding Agents

2. Things That Help Us Rise

    Yeasts, Sodas, & Morning Prayers

3. Things That Sweeten Us

    Alternative Sugars

4. Important Herbs & Spices

    Part Two: The Healing Plate

5. Mealtime Prayers

6. Relishes, Sauces, Salads, & Soups

7. Snacks and Dips

8. Curries, Lentils, Meats, & Beans

9. Noodles, Rice, Breads & Crusts

10. Desserts

Part Three: The Healing Home

11 Good Clean Living

Part Four: The Healing Lifestyle

12 Daily Practices

13 Hormone Balancing Practices

14 Healing Waters

15 Bedtime Practices and Prayers

References

Preface

Everyone needs a hand to hold on to. It's not just a great Mellencamp song; it's the truth. I remember my first trip to a health food store. I remember holding Grandma Kathy's hand as she introduced me to a Health Food Store for the first time. She bought me raw honey candy. I was sold.

I also remember my second trip to a health food store. I was terrified—no health insurance. Sick me—sick baby. Overwhelmed and dirt broke, I poured through the glass doors and to the merciful feet of a medicine woman named Sparrow. She helped me navigate the weird smells and unfamiliar names. She sent me home with $20 worth of vitamins, $5 in tea, and just enough hope to give it a go. It worked!

Since then, I've been a lifelong student of the relationship between food and healing.

These recipes are collected from my life. One section is the sharing and healthy exploration of my Great Grandma's, Grandma's, and Mother's recipes.

Don't worry; you will be prepared with a good choice no matter who comes to dinner!

I am a Nutritionist and Naturopath, and if I've learned anything, it's that wheat and sugar can cause inflammation and feed disease. Wheat is not what it used to be, and just thinking about sugar hurts my pancreas (for more, I suggest the book Wheat Belly by William Davis, MD.).

Hippocrates, regarded as the Father of Modern Medicine, is attributed with the saying, "Let food be thy medicine and medicine be thy food." We are taking him up on that. I have brought healing to my body by following this philosophy, and I wouldn't be a very good friend if I didn't share with you what healing foods have been a help. I've kicked out grains, sugar, dairy, and refined and fried foods.

Beyond these steps, and as much as I would have liked to avoid it, I've even added cold-water fish to my diet twice a week. Fish! This is an example of food as medicine: I may not like it, and it might freak me out, but it's good for me.

If left to my own devices, I'd likely be vegan. However, when I studied nutrition, I was inspired by Weston Price (founder of the Weston Price Method), who described some animal products as "Sacred Food." Price studied human health generationally and tracked the transition from local fresh food to packaged processed food.

His research took him all over the world, and the culmination of it was the theory that a Vegetarian diet was the optimal diet. However, he found that even in primarily vegetarian cultures, each had what he dubbed a "Sacred Food," which was given to people in deep need of support (such as if people were sick, aged, or pregnant). Those Sacred Foods were all animal products, primarily butters and broths, but animal products nonetheless. This concept of Sacred Food gave me comfort in including meat products sparingly in my diet.

The best studies I found for my autoimmune system suggested cold-water fish twice a week. So, that's what I've done (in addition to many other inclusions). Indeed, I want to share my results with as many people as possible, and this book is meant to be a launching pad to that total wellness.

What goes in a healing food pantry?

I was an adult before anyone began to teach me about healthy and healing foods. Perhaps, like younger Shannyn, no one has clued you into the world of ancient grains or low glycolic sugars. Well, consider yourself about to be clued IN! Let's explore!

But first, let's pray.

This is the prayer I say after waking and before getting out of bed.

Lord,

I offer myself to you to do with and build with as you will.
Take away my difficulties that victory over them will stand as a testament to your love, your power, and your way of life.
Strengthen me as I go from here to do your will.

In Jesus' name.
Amen

Part One: The Healing Kitchen

Now the Lord God had planted a garden in the east, in Eden; and there he put the man he had formed. 9 The Lord God made all kinds of trees grow out of the ground—trees that were pleasing to the eye and good for food.
Genisis 2:8

1. Things That Bind

In addition to all these things *put on* love, which is the perfect bond of unity.

Colossians 3:14

All About Eggs

The egg is iconic. It stands as a time-tested symbol of fertility and rebirth. It speaks to abundance and provision. Eggs are more than a protein, they are a whole vibe. The egg is having one of her most historic moments now. In addition to a shortage and rising egg prices, the home chicken trend has reentered the zeitgeist. We had a brief stint with a small brood during the COVID-19 lockdowns. Let's say it wasn't for me. The minute my ex walked out the door, my neighbor Amanda, came and scooped up "Pricilla," "Aquilla," and "Austin Powers."

If you have the strength for a raise-it-yourself approach, more Austin Power's to ya. I have happily resigned myself to using store bought eggs.

Are they all the same? No. Are the chickens from home probably more nutritious? Yes. Regardless, chickens are a good source of protein and a staple of many diets.

Many people are sensitive or allergic to eggs. You may want to observe your reactions and decide if eggs are right for you. You can also test egg reactions with an at-home or with an in-office testing kit.

Let's explore how to make the best choice for you in the egg aisle.

Free-range Eggs come from chickens that have access to outdoor areas. A 2013 study from Rutgers University suggests that free-range eggs contain 4-6 times the amount of vitamin D and 7 times the amount of beta carotene as conventional eggs.

Organic eggs come from Free Range chickens, which are also fed organic food and are kept free of pesticides or fertilizers.

Conventional eggs are the least expensive option at the store. They are often less nutritious than other choices; a telltale sign that an egg is lacking in nutrition is if the

shell is fragile and the yolk is very watery. That said, if you are on a budget, go for those eggs. Thank God for those eggs.
And of course...Thank the chickens and the farmers!

Flax Eggs are a vegan option for baking eggs. It is almost a 1:1 substitution, although it is not exact. My editor Stephen, a Vegan chef by hobby, says that flax eggs are effective as a vegan emulsifier.

To make a Flax Egg, mix 1 Tablespoon of Organic Flax Meal to 2.5 Tablespoons of Water (or follow package instructions).

Note: There are no significant nutritional differences between brown and white eggs. You can also substitute applesauce 1:1 for an egg in most baked recipes. This method doesn't work for all recipes but works well for pancakes and sweet breads.

Other Egg Substitutes:
Applesauce: use ¼ cup of applesauce for every one egg in baking.
Pumpkin Puree: use ¼ cup of pumpkin for every one egg in baking.
Sweet Potato Puree: use ¼ cup of sweet potato or yam for every one egg in baking.

Interlude: *The Goose Who Laid the Golden Egg* – An Aesop Fable

There was once a farmer who possessed the most wonderful Goose in all the world, for every morning when he checked the nest, the Goose had laid a glittering golden egg.

The farmer took the eggs to market and sold them. He began to get rich. But soon he grew greedy with the Goose because she gave him only a single golden egg a day. He wanted more.
Then one day, after he had sold the egg of solid gold, the idea came to him that he could get all the golden eggs at once by killing the Goose and cutting it open to retrieve the eggs inside.

But when he slashed the poor Goose, not a single golden egg was inside, and his precious Goose was dead.

Those who have plenty want more and so lose all they have.

Be thankful for what God's given you each day.

Gluten-Free Binding Agents

Gluten isn't very popular these days, but the reason it has been the "bell of the ball" since ancient times is that it binds and stretches. We don't see that same stretch in other grains and must work to replicate it with our chosen flours. Some substances naturally bind and stretch, while others simply break when stretched too far.

Like your pasta dough, **you** will break instead of bend if **you** are not warmed up. If you don't find the very edge of the stretch, you will snap. However, find your edge, relax gently there, and your edge will expand. You can stretch further in your body, your schedule, and your pasta without losing your noodles.

The grocery store aisle is jam-packed with alternative flours. The Gluten-Free category alone can be confusing. There are so many buzzwords, so little time. Every package shouts, "Buy me!" but what's the best choice for you and your hard-earned dollar? Hopefully this chapter will help you decide.

Welcome to the wonderful world of the flours that make those One Egg Noodles so…noodle-tastic, and the thickening agents that make things oh…so…thick!

Arrowroot is a plant-based, gluten-free substitute with thickening characteristics similar to cornstarch. It is odorless, tasteless, and can be used to thicken sauces and gravies.

Tapioca, made from the cassava root, is gluten-free, and maintains a creamy texture even if you use a bit too much.

Potato starch is a gluten-free substitute that benefits people with corn allergies. To use it as a thickener, dissolve some starch in water to form a slurry, then stir it into the sauce until it thickens.

Guar gum is made from endosperm. It is gluten-free, vegan, and keto-friendly. When substituting guar gum for cornstarch, you can use one-eighth of the amount.

Alternative Flours

Almond Flour is made from milled almonds. It substitutes 1:1 with all-purpose flour but needs a binding agent.

Arrowroot flour, also known as arrowroot powder or arrowroot starch, is a very fine white powder similar to cornstarch. It is flavorless and is primarily used to lighten the texture and structure of baked goods.

Arrowroot powder is a healthier alternative to cornstarch; it is harvested from the plant's tubers without harsh chemicals or high heat. Substitute at a 1:1 ratio.

Coconut flour is made from the meat of coconuts. It can be a tricky substitute because it is thicker than wheat flour and retains more liquid. Therefore, it's best to use it in recipes that specifically call for it.

If you are going to use coconut flour as a substitute, you may have to experiment a bit to get the quantities right. The rule of thumb is to use about a quarter of the quantity of regular flour, and you may need an extra egg or a little more liquid.

Einkorn flour is now widely available online and at many health food stores. Einkorn is the closest option we have today to pre-GMO wheat. It is extremely glutenous. If you want to understand what bread used to taste like, I recommend experimenting with Einkorn. However, be warned! It. Is. Not. Cheap (and I want to prepare you for potential sticker shock). But remember how many delicious breads, noodles, and cookies that bag will make. And with one loaf costing $10 at the health food store, a $10 bag of Einkorn flour may become a way to reduce your grocery bill rather than the splurge it might first appear to be.

Oat flour is simply milled or sifted oats. It is a very nutritious option. Oats are a known nervine agent, meaning they have been proven to help regulate the nervous system. When used in baking, they will cause a denser/heavier product. I like to use this with cookies and crackers. It's also nice as part of a blend when baking bread.

Quinoa flour contains complete protein and can be used as a one-to-one substitute for all-purpose flour. However, baked goods made with quinoa flour will have a grainier texture and carry a tiny, nearly undetectable pungency that is a unique characteristic of quinoa.

Rice flour is produced from finely milled white or brown rice. It should not be confused with rice starch (which is used as a whitener in processed foods); rice flour is a popular substitute for wheat flour. Naturally gluten-free, it provides cakes, breads, and biscuits with a light, crumbly texture and can also be used to thicken sauces.
Rice flour can be tricky to work with. It doesn't soak up as much liquid, resulting in dry or crumbly baking. For that reason, it's best to use it alongside another flour as part of a mixture.

Sorghum flour is an ancient, 100 percent whole grain kernel ground into a fine flour. It is usually beige or white in color, "sweet," softly textured (smoother than rice flour), and has a mild flavor.

Spelt flour is widely available. It contains more protein and is more easily digestible than wheat flour. However, it should be avoided if you have Celiac disease or are removing gluten from your diet.

Gluten Free Flour Blend Variations and Tips

1. Use as a 1:1 replacement for flour or all-purpose gluten free flour blends.
2. Gluten-free flour does not rise like regular flour, so you will need to add leavening agents like baking soda and an acid or baking powder. I don't recommend adding those to your main flour; instead, add them when the recipe requires them.
3. For extra binding properties, you can add 1-2 tbsp of flax meal, especially when you don't use eggs.
4. To prevent rancidity, store in the refrigerator for longer periods of time. You can also store a portion of it in an airtight container at room temperature and refrigerate the rest for later use.

Homemade Gluten Free Baking Mix
1 cup brown rice flour
1 cup sorghum flour
2/3 cup cassava flour
2/3 cup arrowroot powder

Directions:
Add ingredients to mixing bowl and mix until fully combined. Store in an airtight container in a cold/dry place.

INTERLUDE-THE STORY OF HUMPTY DUMPTY

The earliest known version was published in Samual Arnold's *Juvenile Amusements* in 1797 with the lyrics:

Humpty Dumpty sat on a wall,

Humpty Dumpty had a great fall.

Four-score Men and Four-score more,

Could not make Humpty Dumpty where he was before.

A manuscript addition to a copy Mother Goose*'s Melody* published in 1803 has the modern version with a different last line: "Could not set Humpty Dumpty up again". It was published in 1810 in a version of *Gammer Gurton's Garland*.. (Note: Original spelling variations left intact.)

Humpty Dumpty sate on a wall,

Humpti Dumpti had a great fall;

Threescore men and threescore more,

Cannot place Humpty dumpty as he was before.

In 1842, James Orchard Haliwell published a collected version as:

Humpty Dumpty lay in a beck.

With all his sinews around his neck;

Forty Doctors and forty wrights

Couldn't put Humpty Dumpty to rights!

Evidence of an alternative American version closer to the modern received rhyme quoted above is given by William Carey Richard in the issue of a children's magazine for 1843, where he comments that he had come across it as a riddle when he was five-years old and that the answer was "an egg".

Humpty-dumpty sit upon a wall,

Humpty-dumpty had a great fall;

All the king's horses and all the king's men

Couldn't put humpty-dumpty together again.

In science, Humpty Dumpty has been used to demonstrate the second law of thermodynamics. This law describes a process known as entropy, which is a measure of the number of specific ways a system may be arranged and often interpreted as a measure of "disorder. " The higher the entropy, the greater the disorder. After his fall and subsequent shattering, the inability to put him together again represents this principle, as it would be highly unlikely (though not impossible) to return him to his previous state of lower entropy, since the entropy of an isolated system never decreases.

It's a sad story, no matter how you look at it. Perhaps it serves as an allegory for the siege engine used in the English Civil War. Some argue that it's a tale about standing up or seeking help. I remember learning this story in kindergarten. I also recall being of nursery rhyme age when it struck me. I identified with Humpty Dumpty. Even at five years old, I felt I had moved so far from my original self that I couldn't return. I recognized there was no going back. The profound truth that "all the king's men" couldn't put Humpty together again resonated deeply with me. What I didn't know then was that the King not only could restore, but that he absolutely would.

Thank you, King Jesus.

Rice Binds Us

Enriched white rice shouldn't be your first choice; it is essentially sugar. It's commonly found in most food deserts and is often provided at pantries. That being said, thank God for even this rice. If it's your only option, enjoy it. I encourage you to keep your eyes and mind open to trying less processed and more nutritious rice alternatives! When cooking this rice, your ratio of Rice to Water is 1 to 1.

To Make White Rice
1. Boil 1 Cup of Water to 1 Cup of Rice.
2. Add Rice and bring back to boil.
3. Stir.
4. Reduce heat to low and cover.
5. Keep an eye on it and stir occasionally.
6. Cook until rice is soft. (time depends on volume of rice)

Brown Rice is what Enriched White Rice looks like before they polish the nutrition right out of it. (This is oversimplified, but it's true.) You'll need more water and time with brown rice, but it's worth the wait.

To Make Brown Rice
1. Boil 1 ¼ cups of water for 1 cup of short-grained brown rice, or 1 ½ cups of water for 1 cup of long-grained brown rice.
2. Bring the water and rice to a boil in a pot, then reduce heat, cover, and simmer.

You can freeze leftover rice and heat it on the stove with a bit of water! Avoid waste and enjoy a delicious meal later.

Basmati rice is nutty and buttery. Both white and brown Basmati rice use a 1 to 1½ cups ratio. Basic rice can be made by adding water and rice to a pot, bringing it to a boil, then reducing the heat to low and covering it. Stir occasionally to prevent sticking to the bottom.

Jasmine Rice is the yummy, fragrant sister of White Rice. It is widely served in Asian restaurants, especially Thai restaurants, as that is where it originates. Jasmine Rice uses a 1 ½ water radio.

To Make Jasmine Rice
1. Add rice and water to pot.
2. Bring to a foamy boil.
3. Reduce to low heat and Cover.
4. Simmer on low until the water has evaporated and the rice is soft. Monitor the pot and stir occasionally to prevent the rice from sticking to the bottom of the pan.

Wild Rice is not actually rice; it's a type of grass. But what a tasty and nutritious grass it is! Nutty, delicious, and easy to cook, cooked wild rice has about 30% fewer calories and approximately 40% more protein than cooked brown rice. It's also packed with zinc, potassium, and fiber. Wild Rice uses a ratio of 1 to 1 or 1 to 2 cups, depending on how soft you want your finished rice.

To Make Wild Rice
1. Place wild rice, water (or broth), salt in a saucepan with a cover over medium-high heat.
2. Put the lid on and allow it to come to a boil.
3. Reduce heat to low and let it simmer for 40-45 minutes. You will know that it is cooked when some of the grains are popping open.

Cauliflower Rice is a new and exciting binding agent! It's not technically rice, but it's definitely delicious. It's true. Those keto geniuses have found a way to give us a carby-feeling feast with no carbs or sugar spike whatsoever! Meet Cauliflower. The bestie of Broccoli is now appearing as rice (and pizza crust). It's like the other veggies aren't even trying.

To Make Cauliflower Rice
1. Use Cauliflower (organic is ideal)
2. Wash and remove the leaves and stem.
3. Let as much water drain as possible.
4. Ruff-chop Cauliflower into 1- or 2-inch chunks
5. Fill a food processor halfway and pulse the pieces. They will be small at the bottom, so be careful while doing this, but stir those bottom pieces up and pulse again. Repeat until you have riced all of the cauliflower.
6. This will be cooked on the stove top over medium-high heat with oil or medium and a covered pan with some water or broth.

Pro-Tip! You can freeze the raw cauliflower rice for up to three months. So, if you find a great sale, make a few batches and freeze some.

You can also now find cauliflower rice in the frozen food sections of most grocery stores!

Grandma Mary's Syrian Rice
1. Begin by melting a pad of vegan butter or olive oil (or both) in the bottom of a saucepan.
2. Add diced onion to the melted/warmed oil and stir to coat.
3. Reduce to medium-low and allow the onion to brown.
4. Grandma also added vermicelli noodles to the pan and browned them. Rice vermicelli noodles would be a wheat substitution.
5. When the noodles and onion are golden brown, add the broth (Grandma used chicken stock) to the pan, stir, and bring to a boil.
6. Stir in rice (Grandma used Basmati), reduce heat to low, and cover.
7. Simmer low until the liquid is almost gone.
8. Add ½ cup of frozen green peas.
9. Cover again and cook until liquid is gone, and rice is soft.
10. Serve with a pad of vegan butter on top or drizzle with oil. Sprinkle with paprika.

This is often served with green beans and Syrian red sauce.

2 Things That Help Us Rise

The kingdom of heaven is like leaven, which a woman took and hid in three sata of flour until it was all leavened.

Matthew 13:33

Oxford Dictionary

leavening

/ˈlev(ə)niNG/

Noun: leavening; plural noun: leavenings
1. Substances used in dough or batter to make it rise, such as yeast or baking powder.

During the 18th century, yeast was abandoned as a leavening for fruit cakes"

2. A quality or element that permeates and modifies or transforms something for the better.

"underneath the frills and fuss there's a leavening of serious intent"

leav·en /ˈlevən/

verb
1. Cause (dough or bread) to rise by adding yeast or another leavening agent.

"it only takes a little bit of yeast to leaven the bread"

Middle English: from Old French levain, based on Latin levamen 'relief' (literally 'means of raising'), from levare 'to lift'.

Use over time for: leavening.

What is Yeast?

Yeasts are eukaryotic, single-celled microorganisms classified within the kingdom Fungi. The first yeast appeared hundreds of millions of years ago, and currently, at least 1,500 species are recognized.

Baker's yeast was unknown when it was first used to make bread; the earliest definite records date back to Ancient Egypt. Researchers speculate that a mixture of flour and water was left out longer than usual on a warm day, causing the yeasts in the flour's natural contaminants to ferment before baking. The resulting bread would have been lighter and tastier than the previous hard flatbreads.

It is generally assumed that the earliest forms of leavening were likely very similar to modern sourdough. The leavening action of yeast would have been discovered from its action on flatbread doughs, which would have been either cultivated separately or transferred from batch to batch using previously mixed ("old") dough. Leavened bread seems to have developed near the advent of beer brewing, as barm (from the beer fermentation process) can also be used in bread making.

Nutritional yeast is produced by culturing yeast in a nutrient medium for several days. The primary ingredient in this growth medium is glucose, typically sourced from either sugarcane or beet molasses. Once the yeast is ready, it is killed by heat, then harvested, washed, dried, and packaged. Nutritional yeast is a deactivated (i.e., dead) yeast sold commercially as a food product. It is available in the form of yellow flakes, granules, or powder and can be found in the bulk aisle of most health food stores. It is particularly popular among vegans and serves as a significant source of several B-complex vitamins, along with trace amounts of various other vitamins and minerals.

Nutritional yeast has a strong, nutty, or cheesy flavor, which makes it popular as a cheese substitute. It is often used in place of cheese in mashed and fried potatoes, scrambled tofu, or popcorn!

About Baking Soda

Baking soda (aluminum-free) is available at all health food stores and online. Can we take a moment to appreciate the GOAT? Baking soda serves as a cleaning agent, whitening agent, and the hero of the 4th Grade Science Fair Volcano. It is also a leavening agent, but it is so much more. Baking soda got its start 4 million years ago when salt lakes around the world evaporated and created trona deposits.

Trona is a rock that is processed into soda ash (sodium carbonate), a naturally occurring mineral. Soda ash can then be further processed to produce baking soda. The largest deposit of trona in the world is located in Wyoming.

Baking soda is sodium bicarbonate that didn't appear in kitchens until 1848. It's the brainchild of brothers-in-law Dr. Austin Church and John Dwight, who teamed up to distribute their product. Made in Dwight's kitchen, it was called Arm & Hammer Church & Co's bicarbonate of soda. By 1860, Arm & Hammer aimed to show the public just how versatile the ingredient was. They began distributing mini cookbooks filled with family recipes. Are you old enough to remember the television commercial from 1972 that advised Americans to keep a box in their refrigerator? That was a game changer for baking soda. The rest is literally history.

When used in baking, baking soda acts as a chemical leavener. When it reacts with an acid (like vinegar), it produces carbon dioxide, which causes bubbles to rise, helping the cake or cookie rise.

About Baking Powder

Baking Powder (aluminum free) can be found at all health food stores and online. Baking Powder is baking soda plus cream of tartar. It is 3 or 4 times more potent than baking powder.

To make Baking Powder:

1 part baking soda

1 part corn starch

2 parts cream of tartar

Cream of Tartar is a fine, white powder derived from tartaric acid, a natural byproduct of winemaking. It consists of the acid sediment remaining after the wine is poured out.

Cool, huh? Philippians 4:13-14 states, "I've learned by now to be quite content whatever my circumstances. I'm just as happy with little as with much, with much as with little."

A Confession

I paid $8 for six slices of GF sourdough bread, week after week. It's delicious and also gluten-free. Yet, making your own starter and baking this bread is easy! So, there's no reason to fork over your hard-earned dough like I did.

How to Make a Sourdough Starter

Supplies & Ingredients

One big glass jar, tea towel, rubber band

¼ cup of gluten-free flour (I personally use Bob's Red Mill 1:1 Gluten-Free Flour)

¼ cup of pure, clean water (not tap; the chemicals interfere with your starter)

Instructions

Day 1: Mix Flour and Water Together

1. Mix 1/4 cup flour and 1/4 cup filtered water.
2. Stir vigorously, scraping down the sides and incorporating everything.
3. Place a clean tea towel over the bowl and set aside for 24 hours.

Day 2: Discard Some Starter and Feed

1. Discard half of the mixture.
2. Add 1/4 cup gluten-free flour and 1/4 cup water, stir vigorously, and cover.
3. Set aside for 24 hours.

Day 3, 4, & 5: Discard Some Starter and Feed

1. Repeat the day two instructions for days 3-5.
2. Cover and set aside for 24 hours.

Day 6 & 7: Repeat with Increased Frequency

1. On days six and seven, do the same discarding and feeding as you've done on other days, but feed it every 12 hours instead of every 24.

By day seven, your starter should contain enough wild yeast and beneficial bacteria to bake with it.

Rising with Prayers

In the morning, when I rise,
Give me Jesus. Afro-American Hymn
Rev. Jacob Knapp
Author, *Give Me Jesus*, 1845

1 In the morning when I rise,
In the morning when I rise,
In the morning when I rise,
Give me Jesus.
Refrain:
Give me Jesus,
Give me Jesus.
You may have all the rest,
Give me Jesus.
2 Dark midnight was my cry,
Dark midnight was my cry,
Dark midnight was my cry,
Give me Jesus. [Refrain]
3 Just about the break of day,
Just about the break of day,
Just about the break of day,
Give me Jesus. [Refrain]
4 Oh, when I come to die,
Oh, when I come to die,
Oh, when I come to die,
Give me Jesus. [Refrain]
5 And when I want to sing,
And when I want to sing,
And when I want to sing,
Give me Jesus. [Refrain]

Upon Rising

Before you put your feet on the floor.

Give thanks.

See your day just as you hope it will go if it goes perfectly.

Take a deep breath.

Stretch.

Cover your day in prayer.

As a wise church lady once said, "Child, a day hemmed in prayer rarely unravels." Jesus woke up before the sun to spend quiet time with God. Waking early is also deeply embedded in yogic practice. Every farmer or fisherman knows that raising early is key and magnificent. You can't pour from an empty cup, so allow God to fill you up in the gentle and creative space that is the moment of awaking.

"I ask myself, does my schedule look like the schedule of someone who wants to spend time with God today?" – Julia Jackman

Lemon Water

They say the people you work with can make or break a job. Do you find that to be true? I can remember working as a breakfast server with a team of women so wonderful that it changed my life forever. The same is true for my current position. The people at Intentional Life Media truly embody the ministry's name. For example, Carollena Nuffer has a lemon tree in her Tucson, Arizona yard and brings fresh lemons to share with the entire office every day. The kingdom of heaven is like Carollena's lemon tree. Before you drink your coffee, drink lemon water. Help your body do its job and reclaim its balance in a very simple way: by drinking hot lemon water!

Lemon water is a super-star of wellness for good reasons.

Here are just a few reasons to take up this early morning practice:

1. Lemon water is a rich source of vitamin C, potassium, calcium, phosphorus, and magnesium. Lemon juice helps protect the body from immune system deficiencies.
2. Drinking warm water with lemon juice every morning helps maintain the body's pH balance.
3. Lemon juice, with its powerful antibacterial properties, helps combat infections.
4. Lemon juice acts as a detoxifying agent.
5. Lemon juice, with warm water, helps increase the body's metabolic rate.
6. Lemon juice is also very effective at cleansing the liver, as it promotes the liver in flushing out toxins.
7. Lemon juice with warm water helps keep the body hydrated, providing electrolytes to the body.
8. Drinking lemon juice with warm water also helps reduce joint and muscle pain.
9. Lemon juice with warm water is also good for your dental health.
10. Lemon juice with warm water helps regulate natural bowel movements.

3 Things That Sweeten

Kind words are like honey, sweet to the soul and healthy for the body

Proverbs 16:24

A Reflection from the Dead of Winter

Outside my window, is a Crabapple tree whose fruit is frozen solid.

They say that the cold brings out the sweetness in fruits-birthing things like ice wine.

I wonder at what temperature this happens with people.

At what point do we sweeten?

When hard pressed by the cold,

what wonderful elixir will come of us?

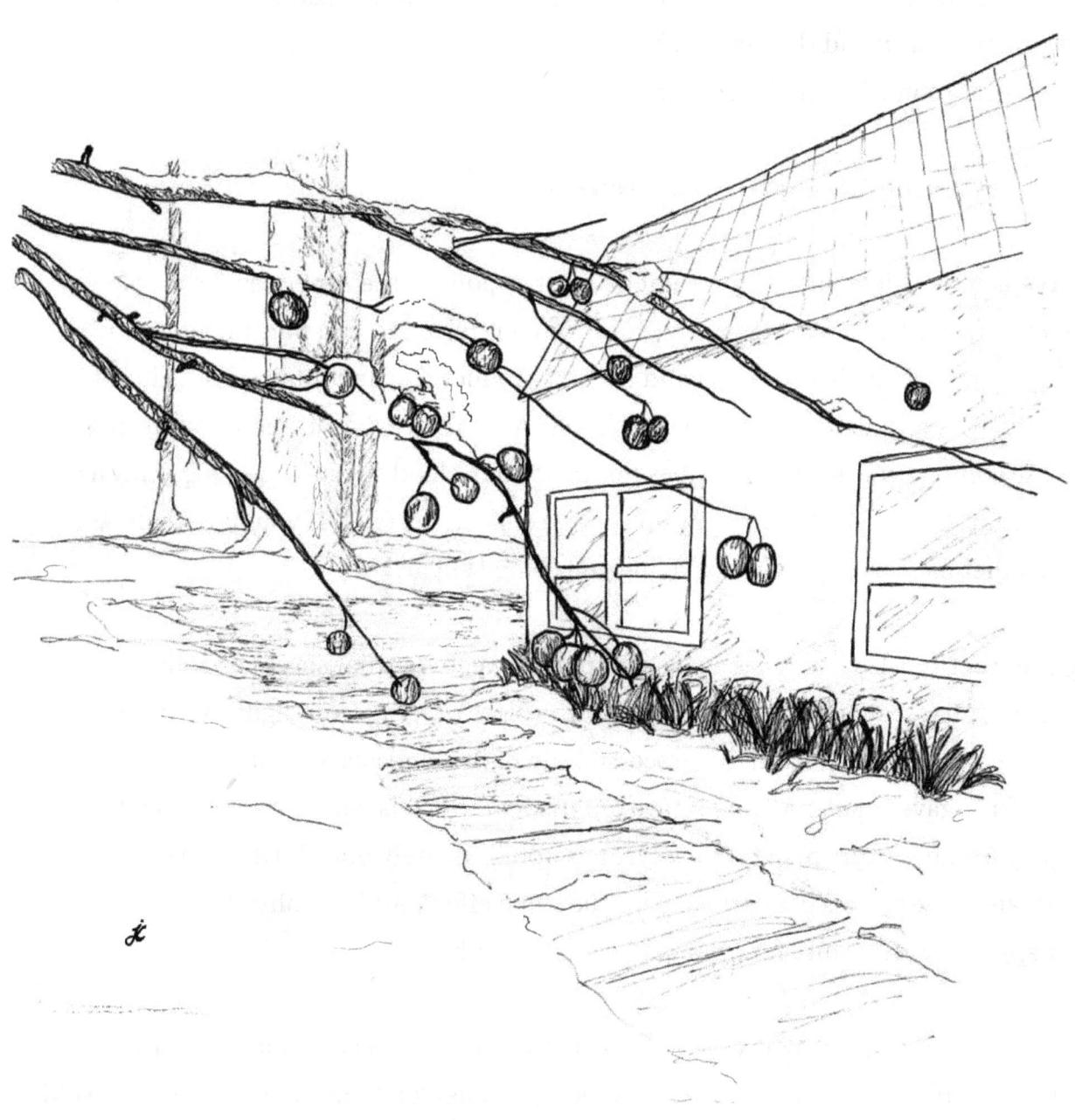

If I've learned anything in Naturopathic College, it's this: white sugar makes us sick. Despite being so sweet and yummy:

Sugar drives Cancer.

Sugar drives Diabetes.

Sugar drives inflammation.

Sugar drives us into a spike and crash.

It's so sweet and yummy.

Thank you, Lord, we have options better than white sugar and saccharine. That is, we have the pink stuff and the blue stuff.

Let's explore some better choices together.

An Overview of Alternative Sweeteners

Agave is a succulent native to several dry, hot regions of the Americas, primarily Mexico and the Caribbean. Agave nectar is often referred to as a natural alternative to sugar, but it is a highly processed and refined product. Sugar contains both glucose and fructose, which can elevate blood sugar levels. Agave syrup has lower amounts of glucose compared to sugar, so it does not raise your blood sugar levels as quickly as table sugar. Consequently, it is low on the glycemic index (GI). If you have diabetes, a low-GI diet may assist you in managing your blood sugar.

Agave nectar, also known as agave syrup, is a sweetener that serves as an alternative to sugar. It has a syrup-like appearance, with colors ranging from light to dark amber. Agave nectar is derived from the processed sap of the blue agave plant (Agave tequila), salmiana (Agave salmiana), and Agave americana, which is commonly referred to as maguey or the century plant. Agave syrup is approximately one-third sweeter than white sugar, allowing for less usage to achieve the same effect. Additionally, it's vegan, making it an appealing substitute for honey for some individuals.

The sap of agave plants, which is toxic to humans if not cooked, is harvested from the heart of the plant. It is then extracted, filtered, and heated to produce the product sold in stores.

Allulose is a naturally occurring sugar found in figs, raisins, wheat, maple syrup, and molasses. It is sweet like table sugar (sucrose) but lacks some of the well-documented downsides of sugar. You can find allulose for sale online and in some retail stores. Because it occurs naturally in very small amounts, the allulose you find packaged for sale is not in its natural form. It has been created artificially by food scientists from fructose (fruit sugar).

At this time, it's considered a "novel food." The FDA has approved it, but the EU has yet to approve it.

Measures 1:1 with white sugar.

Coconut sugar is made by dehydrating coconuts. It's delicious, nutritious, and widely available. It bakes similarly to brown sugar and is a good 1:1 substitution!

Honey is a natural bee product and a wonderful alternative to sugar. Because it's made by bees, if you are baking for a vegan, use maple syrup. But unless you want a vegan choice, honey is a win all day. Honey is one of the most imitated products on the planet, so when you buy honey, choose to purchase it from a reputable source.

Ideally, purchase local honey from a farmer or farmers' market. Local honey has the added benefit of being produced from the co-mingling of local bees and flowers. Those local flowers are the very ones causing us to SNEEZE; therefore, consuming local honey is a well-documented, ancient remedy for hay fever. One tablespoon a day should suffice (less for kids and NONE for babies!).

Maple syrup should always be enjoyed in its natural state. Don't settle for imitations. If you've never tasted real maple syrup, do yourself (literally) the sweetest favor and try it immediately. You'll never be the same. This is simple proof that God loves us and wants us to be happy and healthy. It is nutrient-rich.

1 tablespoon of maple syrup contains about:
- 0.58 milligrams manganese.
- 0.29 milligrams zinc.
- 20 milligrams calcium.
- 42 milligrams potassium.
- 0.02 milligrams iron.
- 4 milligrams magnesium.

It has also been recently shown to contain anti-inflammatory compounds. That's a blessing considering that many sweeteners cause inflammation. If you are working to reduce inflammation, maple syrup may be an excellent choice for you.

Molasses is a thick, dark syrup produced during the sugar-making process. First, the sugar cane is crushed, and the juice is extracted. The juice is then boiled to create sugar crystals, which are removed from the liquid. The thick, brown syrup remaining after extracting the sugar from the juice is molasses. This process is repeated multiple times to generate a different type of molasses each time.

Nutrition note: Unlike refined sugar, molasses contains several vitamins and minerals. One tablespoon has nearly 60 calories and 15 grams of sugar. Key nutrients in molasses include iron, calcium, magnesium, and potassium. Blackstrap molasses, being more concentrated, contains the highest amounts.

Monk Fruit is my current favorite choice; it comes from a small round fruit that is native to China. This granulated sweetener measures and tastes just like white sugar, but without the calories, carbs, or glycemic spike. It is safe for diabetics. It will NOT get golden brown, but DOES have a "Golden" version to substitute for brown sugar in your recipes!

Measures 1:1 with white sugar.

Stevia or **Stevia Rebaudiana** is grown worldwide and is 300 times sweeter than sugar. When you pluck a leaf and taste it, there is no doubt, this is sweet.
You may also experience the aftertaste it's famous for. If not, count it as a blessing, but don't be shocked if you can't slide this health hack under the radar in your bakes. Making stevia extract is similar to brewing tea. You need to steep the steviol glycosides from the leaves. Processors immerse stevia leaves in water and filter out the solids. The filtered stevia liquid is gradually dried to produce stevia powder. Many stevia sweeteners available in stores are stevia-based but contain chemical sweeteners. Look for 100% stevia. The main benefit is its purity, as it causes no spikes in blood sugar.

Honestly, friend, I can't stand the aftertaste. I've tried drops and powders, but can't get past that aftertaste. So, if you enjoy stevia, count those blessings! You can find these drops made from the stevia plant in every flavor. You can substitute them in sparkling water for a sugar-free sweet flavor. You can use the vanilla drops in place of vanilla extract. That is, you can; I cannot because I can't get past the taste. I can't hide it. It will always lead to a sad "what's that funny taste?" look on the face of the excited person tasting my healthy bake. Still, it won't turn your brain to mush like the blue and pink packets they still put on tables today, so it's a better choice all day long. Even though I can't overcome the aftertaste, maybe you don't even notice it. So, while stevia is not for me, you do you, boo.

Xylitol is a sugar alcohol made in Finland from acid-treated birch wood fibers by a chemical process. It is the very definition of processed food, but it also tastes like white sugar.

Measures 1:1 with white sugar.

Be cautious not to overindulge in Xylitol. Consuming it in excess can lead to gas and diarrhea. Additionally, it is highly toxic to dogs.

To make Simple Syrup

Make sure to keep stirring the mixure to avoid burning

1 cup of monk fruit or a 1:1 sweetener of your choice

½ cup of water

A itty bitty pinch of Xanthan Gum

Combine the Monk Fruit and Water in a saucepan and cook over Medium/ High heat until the mixture boils. Then, reduce the heat to low and simmer until all the Monk Fruit has dissolved. Remove the pan from heat, and when the liquid is room temperature, sprinkle and stir in the world's smallest pinch of Xanthan Gum.

Pour into ball jar or decanter with an air-tight lid.

Speaking of Syrup: Remember, corn syrup isn't as sweet as it seems. It stops nutrient absorption. Check your gummy vitamins label for corn syrup before buying them.

4 Important Herbs & Spices

You give a tenth of your spices—mint, dill and cumin. But you have neglected the more important matters of the law—justice, mercy and faithfulness.

Matthew 23:23

(This is a direct quote from Jesus. He wants us to be salt)

The Types of Fine Salt

Fine salt consists of very small grains that dissolve easily and can be measured with greater precision. Consequently, it is among the most popular varieties of cooking salt. Typically, it is extracted from salt brines, resulting in a higher yield at a lower cost.

1. Table salt

This is the most commonly used salt for cooking, baking, and last-minute seasoning. Its fine texture and uniform crystal size make it ideal for measuring volume.
Uses: Table use, cooking, baking, and last-minute seasoning.

2. Iodized salt

Iodized salt is simply table salt with added iodine. As iodine deficiency becomes increasingly common, the need to fortify table salt with potassium iodide also rises. Most iodized salt products contain an anti-caking agent to prevent clumping. The presence of iodine and the anti-caking agent can lead to a more metallic taste in the salt.
Uses: Table use, cooking, baking, and last-minute seasoning.

3. Canning and pickling salt

This type of salt is a vital ingredient in the canning and pickling process. It has a finer grain, allowing it to dissolve easily while keeping the produce in excellent condition. There are no anti-caking additives, which means it doesn't flow as freely.
Uses: Canning and pickling produce.

4. Popcorn salt

Popcorn salt is a super-fine salt that perfectly coats freshly cooked savory snacks like popcorn, fries, and corn on the cob. It penetrates all the nooks and crannies for a consistent and delicious salty flavor. You can make popcorn salt easily by grinding sea salt in a coffee grinder
Uses: Last-minute seasoning.

The Functions of Salt in the Human Body

Salt, also known as sodium chloride, comprises about 40% sodium and 60% chloride. It adds flavor to food and serves as a binder and stabilizer. Additionally, it acts as a food preservative, as bacteria cannot thrive in the presence of high amounts of salt. The human body requires a small amount of sodium to conduct nerve impulses, contract and relax muscles, and maintain the proper balance of water and minerals. It is estimated that we need approximately 500 mg of sodium daily for these essential functions. However, excessive sodium in the diet can lead to high blood pressure, heart disease, and stroke. It can also cause calcium loss, some of which may be drawn from bones. Most Americans consume at least 1.5 teaspoons of salt per day, equivalent to around 3400 mg of sodium, which is significantly more than our bodies need.

The Function of Sea Salt

Adrenal Gland Nourishment: Sea salt can provide the adrenal glands with a balance of minerals like sodium and potassium.

Blood Pressure: Sea salt contains sodium, which helps regulate fluid balance and blood pressure. However, excessive sodium intake can lead to high blood pressure, so it is important to consume sea salt in moderation.

Detoxification: Sea salt minerals can help draw out toxins and impurities from the skin.

Digestion: Sea salt aids in the production of digestive enzymes and juices, which facilitate the breakdown and absorption of food.

Electrolyte balance: Drinking salt water in moderation can help restore electrolytes lost due to physical activity, illness, or hot weather.

Hydration: The minerals found in sea salt assist the body in maintaining electrolyte balance, which is crucial for hydration.

Immune System: Sea salt possesses anti-viral properties that can help bolster the immune system.

Respiratory Health: Sea salt can improve respiratory health by clearing phlegm and mucus from the nasal passages. It can also alleviate a sore throat, chest congestion, and other respiratory issues.

Skin Health: Sea salt can promote healthy skin by hydrating it and supplying minerals that support skin cell function.

The Types of Sea Salt

Sea salt is made from evaporated seawater. It can be myriad colors and have various coarseness and flavor depending on where it was gathered.

Additionally, it possesses a more complex flavor profile than other types of salt due to its minerals and nutrients, which produce bolder bursts of flavor. For these reasons, sea salt is often used in gourmet applications.

1. Flake salt

Flake salt is a sea salt variety defined by its ultra-flaky, pyramid-like crystals. These flakes stick to food better, dissolve more quickly, and impart flavor without changing the texture. Flake salt is often used as a finishing salt.

Uses: Finishing for cooking, baking and creating spice blinds.

2. Fleur de sel

Fleur de sel is a delicate salt crystal from coastal Brittany, France. It is harvested with traditional wooden rakes from the top layer of salt evaporation ponds on sunny, dry days. These conditions result in paper-thin, extremely fine, and delicate salt crystals. Since it can only be gathered when the weather is perfect, fleur de sel has a higher price tag. It is typically off-white or blue-grey in color and has a light, briny flavor.

Uses: Table use, finishing for meats and desserts.

3. Celtic grey sea salt (sel gris)
Celtic grey sea salt, also known as sel gris, is harvested using the same techniques as fleur de sel. However, sel gris is collected from a lower depth in the evaporation pool, where it sinks to the bottom and gathers on the clay lining. As a result, this grey salt possesses a higher mineral content. Additionally, it is slightly moist and has a rich salty flavor.

The Types of Rock Salt
Rock salt originates from within the layers of the Earth's surface, requiring extraction from underground salt mines. This type of salt is rich in minerals and offers exciting new flavor dimensions.

1. Himalayan pink salt
With 84 different minerals, Himalayan pink salt boasts a complex, bold, and slightly sweet flavor. Its distinctive color is derived from traces of iron oxide and magnesium. Finer varieties can be used in cooking, while coarser types work well as a finishing salt.
Uses: Table use, cooking, baking, finishing.

2. Kosher salt
Traditionally, kosher salt was used in Jewish cuisine to extract moisture from meat. However, due to its versatility and texture, it is now used across cuisines. Kosher salt grains are large and coarse, making them easy to pick up and sprinkle over food. It adds a strong, briny flavor and crunchy texture to meals.
Uses: Table use, cooking, baking, finishing, curing, and last-minute seasoning.

3. Kala namak salt
Kala namak salt, also known as black Himalayan salt, possesses a distinctive and pungent aroma and flavor. Its high sulfur content gives kala namak a taste and scent reminiscent of eggs. Therefore, it is frequently used in vegan recipes to impart an egg-like flavor.

Uses: Cooking, particularly for vegan dishes.

The Function of Bragg Liquid Aminos

This ingredient is widely available. It tastes like soy sauce (and is made from soy), but it has way less sodium!

The Functions of Black Pepper

Antioxidants: Black pepper contains piperidine, an alkaloid that provides antioxidant properties.

Anti-Inflammatory: Piperidine has been linked to anti-inflammatory benefits.

Antibacterial: Piperidine in black pepper has antibacterial properties and can fight against harmful bacteria.

Blood Sugar: Black pepper may help with blood sugar control.

Bone Health: Black pepper is a good source of manganese, which can help with bone health.

Brain Function: Piperidine can assist with cognitive brain function.

Cholesterol Levels: Black pepper may improve cholesterol levels.

Digestion: Black pepper aids digestion by interacting with digestive enzymes and juices, stimulating the stomach's production of hydrochloric acid.

Gut Health: Black pepper may improve gut health.

Nutrient Absorption: Piperidine helps absorb nutrients like iron and beta-carotene.

Weight Loss: Black pepper's spicy flavor may have a thermogenic effect, helping the body metabolize food and burn calories.

Grandma's Syrian Pepper – Great-Grandma Nora

This recipe was handwritten on the cover of the cookbook my Grandmother Mary gave my Irish/Polish mom when she married my Syrian/English dad. Grandma had a salt shaker with a few grains of rice in it (to keep the salt from clumping) and a pepper shaker, which was filled with what we all called Syrian Pepper.

This pepper mixture was a wonderful gift from my grandma to my mom, which my mom then passed on to me, and now I can share it with you. Enjoy, beloved.

You will need:
2 parts cinnamon (regulates blood sugar)
1 part clove (antifungal)
1 part nutmeg (mood-boosting digestive aid)
1 part allspice (anti-inflammatory, antioxidant)

Directions:
1. Combine all the spices together
2. Serve in a shaker, or other spice container

It's perfect for dipping bread in olive oil or sprinkling over salad (or any other dish you can think of!).

This is more than just a simple pepper mixture. The spices Great-Grandma Nora chose have many healing properties. For details on these ingredients' health properties, see Chapter 4.

She put this stuff on everything. Grandmas are so smart.

The Functions of Cinnamon

Anti-inflammatory: Cinnamon contains antioxidant compounds that can help reduce inflammation.

Antibiotic: The compound cinnamaldehyde found in cinnamon possesses antibiotic properties.

Antimicrobial properties: Cinnamon can inhibit the growth of harmful microbes in the mouth while promoting the proliferation of beneficial bacteria.

Blood Sugar Management: Cinnamon may help lower blood sugar and reduce the risk of type 2 diabetes.

Bone Health: Cinnamon has served as both a spice and an herbal medicine for centuries. It contains essential minerals such as potassium, magnesium, and calcium, which are vital for maintaining heart health and supporting bone strength.

Brain Health: Cinnamon may be beneficial in combating the effects of an aging brain.

Cancer Prevention: Cinnamon may inhibit or halt tumor growth by preventing the formation of new blood vessels.

Cylon Cinnamon: Helps regulate blood sugar.

Dental Hygiene: Cinnamon can help prevent cavities, tooth decay, and bad breath.

Gut Health: Cinnamon may support gut health.

Heart Health: Cinnamon may help manage blood pressure and protect against heart disease.

The Functions of Clove

Anti-Inflammatory: Cloves contain compounds that can reduce inflammation, which may help with arthritis and other health issues.

Anti-Parasitic: A 2013 Egyptian University study shows a direct antiparasitic effect. The active compounds in **clove** buds are highly anthelmintic (**anti-parasitic**). This can be as simple as chewing cloves instead of chewing gum. Cloves are also extensively used in Chinese and Ayurvedic medicine.

Antimicrobial: Clove oil has antibacterial and antifungal properties that can be used as an antiseptic for oral infections.

Antioxidant: Cloves are full of antioxidants, which can help fight free radicals that damage cells. This may help lower the risk of heart disease, diabetes, and some cancers.

Antiviral: Eugenol, the main active compound in cloves, may help prevent viral replication and reduce the infection of herpes viruses.

Bone Health: Cloves provide a valuable source of manganese, which is vital for bone formation and density.

Liver Health: Cloves may enhance liver function and alleviate symptoms of liver cirrhosis and fatty liver disease.

Pain Relief: Clove oil can numb the affected area and act as a natural analgesic. It can help with toothaches, pain during dental work, and other conditions. Clove can also help babies navigate teething.

The Functions of Coriander

Coriander (*Coriandrum sativum* L., Apiaceae) was first cited in the Ebers papyrus (1550 BC) and is used in both cuisine and traditional medicine. It is primarily cultivated for its yellowish-brown globular fruits, known as coriander seeds. This fast-growing annual herbaceous plant, which originated from the Mediterranean and Middle Eastern regions, is also found in South America, North Africa, and India. Its leaves are commonly referred to as cilantro.

Antioxidant: Polyphenols' most characteristic activities are their antiradical and antioxidant properties. The high amount of polyphenols in *C. sativum* extracts makes it a suitable reducing agent, lipid peroxidation inhibitor, and free radical scavenger.

Detoxifying: Cilantro is widely studied and used as a detoxification agent for heavy metals and liver support. It is also a known diuretic.

The Function of Cumin

Antioxidants: Cumin contains flavonoids that serve as antioxidants, neutralizing free radicals which can cause cell damage. Antioxidants might help prevent diseases such as cancer, heart disease, and high blood pressure.

Nutrients: Cumin is a good vitamin A, calcium, and iron source.

Other Potential Benefits: Cumin may also help reduce oxidative stress, suppress inflammation, and regulate signaling pathways that control cell death.

Traditional Medicine: Cumin and its essential oil have long been used in traditional medicine. In Ayurvedic medicine, cumin was used to treat gastrointestinal distress, diarrhea, and jaundice.

WARNING
Cumin may interact with certain medications, including:

Anticoagulants and Antiplatelet Drugs: Cumin may slow blood clotting, so taking it with these medications may increase the risk of bleeding and bruising.

Diabetes Medications: Cumin may cause blood sugar to drop too low when taken with diabetes medications.

Rifampin: Cumin may increase how much Rifampin the body absorbs, which may increase the effects and side effects of Rifampin.

The Functions of Fennel or Foeniculum Vulgare

Fennel is rich in antioxidant compounds such as rosmarinic acid, chlorogenic acid, quercetin, and apigenin, which may help lower the risk of chronic diseases like cancer and heart disease.

Antibacterial: Fennel has antibacterial properties that can help improve digestion by reducing unwanted intestinal microorganisms.

Blood Pressure: Fennel contains potassium, calcium, and magnesium, which can help lower blood pressure.

Bone and Muscle Health: In addition to calcium and magnesium, fennel also contains iron, which can help prevent osteoporosis, promote strong bones, and help your heart and muscles contract properly.

Digestion: Fennel can help relieve digestive complaints like gassiness.

Hair Health: Fennel seed oil can help strengthen hair follicles, nourish the scalp, and stimulate hair growth.

Immune Support: Fennel contains vitamins C and E, which can help boost the immune system.

Other Health Benefits: Fennel is a traditional herb with a long history of medicinal use. It may assist with weight management, curb appetites, improve anemia symptoms, support breast milk production, alleviate some menopause symptoms, and soothe a sore throat. It can be consumed raw in salads and snacks or cooked in a variety of dishes. Fennel is also used to make herbal teas and spirits.

The Functions of Garlic

Anti-Inflammatory: Garlic contains diallyl disulfide, which can help with sore and inflamed muscles and joints.

Antimicrobial: Garlic can inhibit and destroy bacteria, fungus, and parasites. It can be used to treat conditions like colds, diarrhea, and vaginitis.

Antioxidant: Garlic is a powerful antioxidant that can protect cells from free radical damage.

Blood Pressure: Garlic may help lower blood pressure in people with hypertension.

Cholesterol: Garlic may help lower cholesterol levels.

Immune System: Garlic can help strengthen the immune system.

Liver Protection: Garlic may assist in protecting the liver from damage, particularly from ethanol-related liver injury.

Lymphatic System: Garlic can activate the lymphatic system, which helps the body get rid of waste.

Wound Infections: Garlic can help treat wound infections caused by the common cold, malaria, cough, and pulmonary TB.

The Functions of Onions

Antibacterial: Onions have antibacterial properties and have been used in folk medicine to treat coughs, colds, and catarrh. In traditional medicine, onion juice is dropped into the ear as a remedy for ear infections.

Antioxidants: Onions are rich in antioxidants, which can help prevent cell damage and protect against chronic diseases.

Bone Health: Eating onions may be associated with improved bone density.

Gut health: Onions are high in fiber, which can help maintain gut health.

Detoxification: Onions are rich in amino acids that can aid in detoxifying the body of heavy metals.

Heart Health: Onions contain quercetin, a flavonoid that may help reduce the risk of heart disease by fighting inflammation and lowering cholesterol levels. Onions may also have blood-thinning characteristics.

Immune System: Onions are high in vitamin C, which can help regulate the immune system.

The Functions of Peppermint (Mentha Piperita)

Anti-Inflammatory: Peppermint has anti-inflammatory properties.

Antibacterial, Antifungal, and Antiviral: Peppermint can kill some types of bacteria, fungi, and viruses.

Digestive aid: Peppermint can soothe an upset stomach, aid digestion, and relax the gastrointestinal tract muscles. It's used to treat irritable bowel syndrome (IBS) and indigestion.

Pain Relief: Peppermint oil can be applied topically to relieve pain from headaches, muscle aches, joint pain, and itching. It can also reduce pain sensation in the gastrointestinal tract.

Sinus Relief: Peppermint tea may help relieve clogged sinuses caused by infections, the common cold, and allergies. Peppermint is also used in chest rubs to treat common cold symptoms.

Skin Relief: Peppermint oil can relieve itching caused by bug bites, ivy, hives, and other skin conditions.

The Function of Rosemary

Anti-Inflammatory: Rosemary has anti-inflammatory properties that can help with some inflammatory skin conditions.

Antimicrobial: Rosemary oil has antimicrobial properties that can kill some bacteria and fungi.

Antioxidant: Rosemary contains carnosic acid, a compound with antioxidant properties that can neutralize harmful particles in the body.

Blood Clotting: Rosemary is high in manganese, which helps the body form blood clots and allows injuries to heal faster.

Digestion: Rosemary tea can help with digestion by reducing acid and excess gas.

Hormonal Health: Rosemary can help detox estrogens in the liver, which can be beneficial for women with heavy periods, bad PMS, and other hormonal issues.

Immune System: Rosemary can help lower the risk of infection and help the immune system fight any infections.

Liver Health: Rosemary oil can detoxify the liver and improve gallbladder health.

Memory and Concentration: Rosemary has been used as a memory aid for centuries, and studies have shown that smelling rosemary essential oil can improve cognitive performance.

Stress and Anxiety: Inhaling the smell of rosemary oil may help reduce stress and anxiety.

The Functions of Turmeric

Anti-Inflammatory: Turmeric possesses anti-inflammatory properties. I make an effort to consume it daily. I sprinkle it into my shakes and broths and mix it into my sauces. However, avoid using it in peach pie, as your peaches will turn green (I learned this the hard way).

A bouquet of herbs from Shakespeare

The chain link gate creaked slowly open, arthritic with the ice in its joints, and my rubber boots slushed through the crusty snowy yard. This is nuts, I thought. This is totally crazy. If someone sees me, they will say for sure, "She's bought the farm."

But …as Janice Joplin said, "Freedom's just another word for nothing left to lose" and so I knelt down amongst the herbs, the long-gone sage and thyme and the wilted chives, and brushed the ice and mud-caked leaves away from their roots.

"I've neglected you," I said. "I'm sorry. I will try to do better in the spring." I was talking out loud to plants. The step to talking to Mom and Dad wasn't a large one.

"Mom, Dad," I said, voice desperate, like a child lost in the mall or left behind at the circus. Gazing straight ahead into the midday snow, I squinted my eyes to see if they appeared. Blinded by the golden explosion of sunlight on the glassy drift, I didn't see them, but I still said out loud, "I miss you. I don't know what to do. I don't know how to live. I'm so lost."

I brushed the face of the soft sage brush with the back of my hand, and the plant talked back with a warm waft of oil. "And I'm so sick of crying." I said, lacing my fingers into the bright herbal branches. I squeezed it tight. "Sage is supposed to bring me peace."

I crushed the brown, frozen leaves between my fingers and inhaled deep as I could, filling every corner of my lungs with the smell of sage and snow and tears. "I don't know what to do. Are you there? Where are you? I feel like I'm losing you and I don't know what to do. What if I forget you?"

Then I remembered Ophelia's line, "Here's rosemary, that's for remembrance. I pray you sirs, remember…. Rosemary, for … remembrance."

"Rosemary helps memory," I said. I shook the rosemary bush by the plant's root and snow flew off like water from a just-bathed puppy dog.

From the Healing Season, Page 100 and 101.

Before I became a lover of the Bible, I was a lover of Shakespeare. Shakespeare was quite knowledgeable of herbal medicine and we get this side benefit when reading his works. For example, from a couple of different plays:

Lavender: "Perdita: Here's flowers for you: Hot lavender, mints, savory and marjoram" (*The Winter's Tale*, Act IV, Scene 4).

Chamomile: "Falstaff: For though the chamomile, the more trodden on the faster it grows, so youth, the more it is wasted, the sooner it wears" (*Henry IV*, Act II, Scene 4).

Lemon Balm: "Cleopatra: As sweet as Balm, as soft as air, as gentle" (*Antony and Cleopatra*, Act IV, Scene 2).

Finally, the *Hamlet* scene that makes us all reach for tissues: Ophelia's father, who was just stabbed to death at the hand of her true love, causes her to snap; she breaks. It is known as Ophelia's "Mad Scene." She brings a bouquet of Rosemary, an herb long-used to signify memory:

Rosemary: "Ophelia: There's rosemary, that's for remembrance; pray love, remember."(*Hamlet*, Act IV, Scene 5).

Note: if you are studying for a test, have some rosemary nearby. When you take the test, bring a cotton ball with rosemary oil and inhale its essence to spark your recall.

Mint: "I am that flower. That Mint. That Columbine." (*Love's Labour's Lost*, Act V, Scene 2)

The Elizabethans had many varieties of Mint available, including Spearmint and Garden mint. Mints were used in cooking, toiletries, and as medicinal aids to refresh the mind and strengthen memory.

Lily: "The lily I condemned for thy hand, And buds of marjoram had stol'n thy hair" (Sonnet 99)

Marjoram is related to Oregano and was used as a food seasoning and cooking herb. It was also added to nosegays and washing waters. In ancient times, it formed part of the garlands of newly married couples as a symbol of honor, love, and happiness.

Thyme: "I know a bank where the wild thyme blows." (A Midsummer Night's Dream, Act II, Scene 1).

Wild Thyme has a strong aromatic scent and beautiful pink and purple flowers. Francis Bacon (1561-1626) stated that if your garden had alleys, then they should be planted with fragrant flowers such as *"burnet, wild thyme, and watermints,"* which, when *"trodden upon and crushed,""perfume the air most delightfully."* The Romans used Wild Thyme as a remedy for melancholy and nervous tension. Wild Thyme differs from common garden Thyme (*Thymus vulgaris*), which is smaller and less fragrant.

Chamomile: "For though the camomile [sic], the more it is trodden on the faster it grows, yet youth, the more it is wasted the sooner it wears." (Henry IV, Part 1, Act II, Scene 4).

Chamomile (or camomile) derives its name from the Greek *Chamaimelon*, meaning "earth apple, "because its flowers are said to smell like apples. It was very popular in Elizabethan gardens, favored for its medicinal qualities and fragrance. In *A New Orchard and Garden* (1648), William Lawson wrote, "Large walks, broad and long, close and open, like the Tempe groves in Thessaly, raised with gravel and sand, having seats and banks of Camomile; all this delights the mind and brings health to the body."

Part Two: The Healing Plate

The Lord God commanded the man, saying, "From any tree of the garden you may freely eat;

Genisis 2:16

Excerpt from The Healing Season: How a Deadly Tornado Wrecked and Reshaped My Faith

In the wreckage, I found an almost-complete set of my great grandma's fancy China. It was like an Easter egg hunt, only I was finding eggshell China with roses and a golden stripe. How could this have made it? It was exactly what Mom would have given me if she could only choose one thing; that, and her ring.

I also found her apron, the one she always wore. She got the quilted denim thing at the St. Barbara ladies' bazaar in the 1980s and wore it every time she cooked or cleaned. It was caked, as everything else was, in a spray of mud and dust. I've cleaned it well and wear it all the time, too. To be honest, it's pretty awful. There are many cuter aprons, but I don't care.

Mom's fancy lace tablecloth was there, too, as was her wooden spoon and the cookbook my Syrian grandma had given her when she married Dad. It had her handwritten notes.

This time, I heard Mom's voice. "This is how you will keep us alive. You will make the food and set the table and when you do, you will tell the story of who we were."

From The Healing Season, Page 56

Psalm 146

Praise the Lord.

Praise the Lord, my soul.

I will praise the Lord all my life;

I will sing praise to my God as long as I live.

Do not put your trust in princes,

in human beings, who cannot save.

When their spirit departs, they return to the ground;

on that very day their plans come to nothing.

Blessed are those whose help is the God of Jacob,

whose hope is in the Lord their God.

He is the Maker of heaven and earth,

the sea, and everything in them—

he remains faithful forever.

He upholds the cause of the oppressed

and gives food to the hungry.

The Lord sets prisoners free,

the Lord gives sight to the blind,

the Lord lifts up those who are bowed down,

the Lord loves the righteous.

The Lord watches over the foreigner

and sustains the fatherless and the widow,

but he frustrates the ways of the wicked.

10 The Lord reigns forever,

your God, O Zion, for all generations.

Praise the Lord.

5 Mealtime Prayers

He took the five loaves and the two fish, and looked up toward heaven. He blessed the food and breaking the loaves, He gave them to the disciples, and the disciples gave them to the crowds.

Matthew 14:19

It's been my privilege to be a show host on Family Life Radio for the past 15 years. In 2024 invited my radio listeners and friends to share their mealtime prayers. Here's what they brought to the table. Aren't they delicious?

"Lord, we thank you for the bounty before us and ask that you provide for all who are hungry around the world. Bless the hands that have prepared this meal, may it nourish our bodies, so we have strength to serve You. May all be to the glory of God in Jesus's name, Amen."

- Freida Gupton Adams

"We say a Catholic-Lutheran combo from my childhood: Bless us oh Lord, for these Thy gifts which we are about to receive, from Your bounty through Christ our Lord, Amen. Come Lord Jesus, be our guest and let this food to us be blessed. Amen."

-Candace Decker

"Come Lord Jesus
Be our guest
And let thy gifts
To us be blessed
Amen."

-Shawn Jones MacPhee

"Lord, we thank you for this day. Thank you for the food we have before us and the hands that prepared it. Please bless it to our use and us to your service. In Jesus name, Amen."

-Katie Miller

"God, bless not the food and drink but what we do and what we think. And grant for all our work and play that we may love You more each day."

-Kindra Silk Kreislers

"Dear Lord, Bless us sinners while we eat our dinners. Amen."

-Andrea Gregory

"Thank you, Jesus, for this food. Amen!"

-Sadie Jones

"Dear Lord, thanks you for this time to gather together. Please let this food nurture us and bless us deeply. We are grateful."

-Courtney Crum

"Thank you, God for the food before us, the family and friends beside us and the love between us."

-Faith Simsick

"For food in a world where many walk in hunger,
For faith in a world where many walk in fear,
For family in a world where many walk alone.
We give thanks, O Lord
Amen"

-Criss Nagy Tolliver

"Thank you, God, for giving us food
Thank you, God, for giving us friends
For the food we eat, for the friends we meet
Thank you, God, for giving us food."

-Dawn Miller

"God is great, God is good. Let us thank Him for our food By His hand, we all are fed. Give us Lord our daily bread. Amen."

-April Moore Aftanas

"Be present at our table Lord. Be here and everywhere adored. These morsels bless and grant that we may feast in paradise with thee."

- Mary Quinlan

(Indeed, this is the first prayer I taught my children & grandchildren. My grandmother taught it to me).

"Bless us O Lord and these Thy gifts from which we are about to receive from Thy bounty through Christ our Lord. In the name of the Father and of the Son and of the Holy Spirit. Amen."

- Timm Allen

"I've got food on the table. Lord I know you are able."

- Tauren Wells

Thank you for this meal, and thank you for our love. Amen.

- My Family's Table

Thank you, God. Thank you, God. Thank you, God.

- Me

Before you spend your cheddar on building Your Healing Pantry:

Hey, friend!
Building a pantry and filling a kitchen with the right pots, pans and tools for the job can be expensive and overwhelming. Here are a couple suggestions that might help:

Avoid pots and pans with Teflon coating, which is linked to hormone disruption. Opt for stainless steel or good cast iron pans, which can add iron to your cooking. Check your library and see if it has a kitchen lending library. My local library, and perhaps yours, has an arsenal of blenders, mixers, specialty cake pans, and cookie sheets. They even had a donut baking pan! Before you spend your money on making ONE Bundt cake a year, why not just borrow that pan when you're picking up your summer read?

Before investing in a food dehydrator, why not check one out from your local lending library and try the Flax Bread recipe?

Also, check for a Seed Library! You may also be able to source all the seeds needed to grow your fresh herbs or greens!

6 Soups, Salads and Sauces

Therefore I tell you, do not be anxious about your life, what you will eat or drink, nor about your body, what you will put on. Is not life more than food, and the body more than clothing? Look at the birds of the air: they neither sow nor reap nor gather into barns and yet your heavenly Father feeds them. Are you not of more value than they?

Matthew 6:25-26

Remember, as with all recipes, if your Great-Great-Grandma wouldn't recognize it as food, don't eat it! Enjoy these heirloom recipes with love from my Irish Grandmas, Kay and Kathleen, my Syrian Grandma, Mary, my mom, Jacque, and me.

CHOW CHOW – Aunt Eunice

Does your family have an Aunt who is not blood related but is as much a part of your family as the ones who show up on Ancestry.com? Our Irish, Polish family was blessed with our Italian Aunt, Eunice.

Eunice was a widow and mother of two beautiful daughters. They were family as well. Aunt Eunice worked as the lunch lady at our school, Holy Spirit Central. Everyone wanted to be a hot lunch kid during the "Eunice Era. " One of her tricks was to rub the inside of your salad bowl with raw onion and then freeze the bowl. When you tossed your salad, it would be cold, crisp, and have a little hint of onion. Eunice was a genius. This is her go to salad, the very best of what was around.

You will need:
1 peck cucumbers (12-13 lbs.)
2 large cauliflowers
4 onions
12 peppers (green and red) – Eunice meant Bell, but if you're in New Mexico and have chilies, use what YOU have!

To Make:
1. Chop the cucumbers
2. Cube the cauliflower
3. Chop the onions
4. Chop the peppers
5. Add 2 cups salt. Let stand overnight.
6. Drain with cloth sack.
7. Heat 1 gallon vinegar and thicken with ½ lb. of dry mustard, 1 oz. of turmeric, ¾ oz. of curry powder, 6 tablespoons flour (or g. flour, spelt, einkorn) and 1 teaspoon red pepper. If you care for sweetness, you can add sugar to taste (Eunice was diabetic and LOVED sugar. In her honor, I sub with monk fruit).

8. Add cucumbers, cauliflower, onions, and peppers to liquid and cook until onions are transparent.

Note: DANG, these grandma recipes create large batches! I believe that is part of the secret to HOW they thrived with little. They truly lived LARGE. They produced massive seasonal batches and then canned and froze them. As you approach your plan, think about how you can scale it and preserve what you create.

Cranberry Orange Relish – Mom

My mom taught me to prepare this dish with granulated sugar. Although she couldn't eat it because of her diabetes, it was my favorite. Now, my daughter, like her mother, shares it as a must-have at Christmas and Thanksgiving feasts.

You will need:
1 bag of cranberries
2 whole oranges
½ cup granulated sweetener or honey (more to taste)

Directions:
1. Wash berries
2. Quarter oranges and remove seeds
3. Peel the oranges if you don't like the bitterness of the rind. Add orange zest if rind is removed.
4. Add all ingredients to a food processor and pulse to desired consistency.

Grandma Mary's Salad

You go to a Middle Eastern restaurant and are served the most perfect salad. Sometimes it's called House Salad, sometimes it's called a Fattoush salad. It's addictive in the very best way. How do they do it? Wonder no more.

For Fattoush salad, you will need:
3 medium tomatoes
1 large cucumber
½ head of Romain lettuce
1 small white onion
1 teaspoon dry mint, crushed (or 1 tablespoon fresh chopped mint)

For the dressing, combine and drizzle:
2 tablespoons olive oil
Juice of one lemon
Salt to taste

Cucumber & Tomato Salad – Grandma Mary

The summertime meant a trip to visit Grandma outside Detroit. It was bliss. Grandma could grow anything and everything. Behind her garage was a patch of cucumbers and tomatoes, a bed of mint, and a wall of grapes for grape leaves. We could sit in the dirt, pick, and snack. With hearts and bellies full, we'd retreat to her matchbox of a kitchen and make this heirloom salad to share with the cousins.

Years later, it would be my honor to serve with the Syrian American Rescue Network, helping refugees resettle. A dainty young mother named Fazel and her family had fled war-torn Homs. She would reminisce about her cucumber garden and gush about her tomatoes like they were Damascus roses. This recipe held her together.

For the salad, you will need:

3 medium tomatoes diced or in wedges

2 cucumbers diced or sliced

For the Dressing You will need:

½ Tablespoon parsley chopped

2 cloves of garlic, diced.

½ hot pepper diced

Juice of one lemon

3 Tablespoons of olive oil

Salt to taste

Toss and serve cold. You can add feta, vegan feta, or black olives with more parsley to garnish.

This is a perfect salad served with Mujaddara!

Tabbouleh – Grandma Mary

Don't tell my Grandma, but I've replaced some of her ingredients in this recipe with healthier substitutions.

You will need:
½ cup burghul wheat (sub ½ cup quinoa), cooked
2 large tomatoes, diced
1 bunch of green onions, chopped
4 bunches of parsley, chopped
½ bunch of chopped mint or 2 tablespoons diced mint (pro-tip-mint tea is dried mint and you and use this in a pinch)
1 large cucumber, peeled and chopped
½ cup olive oil
Juice of three lemons
1 tablespoon salt (to taste)
½ teaspoon black pepper

Directions:
1. Clean, stem, and chop all herbs
2. Combine all ingredients
3. Enjoy!

Sauces

Catsup - Great Grandma Kay

With a bottle of Catsup with suspicious ingredients ringing in at almost $6, why not make your own with items you likely have on hand already?

You will need:
2 (28 ounce) cans crushed tomatoes
½ cup water, divided
⅔ cup granulated sweetener
¾ cup distilled white vinegar
1 teaspoon onion powder
½ teaspoon garlic powder
1 ¾ teaspoons salt
⅛ teaspoon celery salt
⅛ teaspoon mustard powder
¼ teaspoon finely ground black pepper
¼ teaspoon cayenne pepper, or to taste
1 whole clove

Directions
1. Cook on high in crockpot with top off until it's reduced by ½ (About 8-10 hours).
2. Still each hour.
3. Blend with an immersion blender and then ladle into strainer to remove seeds.
4. Pour into glass bowl or bottle.
5. Cover and Cool.

Grandma's Syrian Red Sauce – Grandma Mary

Every culture seems to have one. A tomato-based sauce that is a family staple. Don't you just love that? When I was in Ghana on a Compassion trip, they served this red sauce with a kiss of curry. In Italy we know it better with oregano and basil. I love the abundance and creativity simmering in every pot. Since the first tomato back in Adam and Eve's Garden to now. Every tomato so packed with seed that each of us could become tomato farmers. Plus you can thank them for the heart healthy they bring. God just love us. Clearly. He wants us to be healthy.

You will need:
1 small onion, chopped
2 cloves of garlic, chopped
¼ cup olive oil
2 cups of tomato juice
5 ripe tomatoes, finely chopped (optional)
¾ teaspoon salt
1/3 teaspoon pepper
1/3 teaspoon allspice
¼ cup dry red wine

Directions:
1. Sauté onion and garlic in oil.
2. Add tomato juice, wine, salt, and spices to onions.
3. Cover and simmer over low heat for 30 minutes.
4. Serve over rice or green beans.

Optional: Garnish with a drizzle of olive oil, toasted pine nuts, and browned onion.

GARLIC GARIC GARLIC DRESSING – Shauun Baker

Dayton, Ohio, in the 80s and 90s, was home to an Italian restaurant with the most garlicky salad dressing on planet Earth. My friend group consisted of a pack of stage actors who would go out for Domic's house salads. If we were doing a play at the time, the rule was, "everyone eats it or no one eats it," because the resulting garlic breath was intense. Read about the properties of garlic, and you'll see why we never got sick. Once, I begged our server for the recipe. She told me the secret was using dried garlic. She was either a dirty liar or a great gatekeeper. Either way, Domic's has been closed for decades, but my friend Shaunn sweet-talked that former server into sharing the recipe. She said the secret was squeezing the oil out of the freshest cloves. Shaunn's recipe is a perfect facsimile. He should be a spy.

You will need:

½ cup red wine vinegar

1/3 cup olive oil or oil of your choice

1/8 cup granulated sweetener 1:1 substitute of your choice

2 oz. jar pimento

5 cloves of fresh garlic, pressed

Directions:
1. Put all ingredients in a blender and blend to desired texture.

This is a nice and easy recipe and makes a great marinade for grilling vegetables.

Tahini Sauce – Great Grandma Nora (Adapted)

You will need:

1 cup tahini

½ cup cider vinegar

½ cup water

2 cloves of garlic crushed

¼ cup Bragg aminos

½ teaspoon sea salt

¼ cup parsley

Directions
1. In a bowl, mix tahini with all other ingredients.
2. Add enough water to make a thick sauce.
3. Optional: pour into a blender and blend until smooth.

This is fantastic on everything: over meat, fish, tofu, salad, steamed or roasted vegetables, or even by the spoonful! I won't judge.

Pesto – Grandma Kathy

You will need:

3 cups fresh basil leaves

1 ½ cups chopped walnuts, pine nuts, or pistachios (whatever you have on hand)

4 cloves garlic, peeled

¼ cup grated vegan parmesan cheese

1 cup olive oil

Salt and pepper to taste

Directions:
1. Wash basil and remove leaves from the stems. Discard stems (keep them to add a tang to broth at a later time!)
2. Add all ingredients (except oil) to a food processor
3. Blend while slowly drizzling in oil until smooth.

You can keep this in your refrigerator or freeze cubes for quick use in the future on pizza crust, pasta, toast, or roasted veggies.

Soups

In the autumn and winter, it's like an internal clock ticks. It's soup season. Warming. Easy to digest. Strangely nostalgic. Soup is, in fact, good food. It's easy to prepare ahead. You can freeze it, can it, or give it away as gifts. Soup for the win. So here are some of my winning soups for days when you need something simple and 'oh-so-good.'
When the kids need to get to school, you have to get to work. Everyone rushes to after-school events. When are you supposed to find time to have dinner together, let alone cook?

Prep these ingredients and place them into the freezer for when someone from your community needs a blessing.

There is nothing like a good ol' fashioned meal train when you are struggling.

Crockpot Minestrone Soup

You will need:

1 (28 oz) can diced tomatoes

4 cups broth

1 medium baking potato, peeled and diced

1/2 cup onion, chopped

1/2 cup carrot, chopped

1/2 cup celery, chopped

1/4 teaspoon ground black pepper

1 (16 oz) can cannellini beans, rinsed

1 medium size zucchini, diced

1 cup frozen cut green beans, thawed

1/3 cup pesto (recipe on page 88)

Directions:
1. Mix tomatoes, onion, carrot, celery, and black pepper into a 4-quart or larger crockpot.
2. Cover and cook on LOW for 7 to 9 hours, or until vegetables are tender.
3. Stir in the cannellini beans, zucchini, and green beans.
4. Cover and cook on HIGH for 15 minutes, or until zucchini is tender.
5. Spoon into bowls and top with pesto.

I discovered this recipe on the back of a can of cannellini beans in 1990. I wish I could recall the brand to give credit.

Note on canned foods: research indicates the aluminum in the can may be harmful. Look for lined canned foods or choose glass or dried when possible.

Crock Pot Corn Quinoa Chowder – Mom

You will need:

3/4 cup quinoa

1 - 2 tablespoons olive oil

2 medium potatoes

16 oz package frozen corn kernels or 4 ears fresh corn on the cob

4 cups vegetarian soup stock or water

1 cup chopped green beans

1 celery stalk, diced

1/2 large red pepper, diced

2 - 3 cloves garlic

1/2 teaspoon ginger

1/2 jalapeno pepper, seeded

1 teaspoon ground coriander

1 teaspoon paprika

1/2 teaspoon dried oregano leaf

1/2 teaspoon dried thyme leaf

1 bay leaf

Salt to taste

Fresh ground black pepper to taste

2 Tbsp chopped cilantro or 2 scallions sliced

For added spice: Add 1/8 - 1/4 teaspoon chipotle pepper powder

Directions:
1. Soak the quinoa for 5 minutes
2. Rinse, then drain into a colander
3. Peel and mince the garlic, jalapeno, and ginger
4. Wash and trim the celery, slice lengthwise, then crosswise to dice
5. Seed and dice the red pepper
6. Peel and chop the potatoes into bite-sized pieces

7. If using fresh corn, peel and slice the kernels off the cobs
8. Combine all ingredients except corn, cilantro, scallions in a large crockpot
9. Cover and cook on low for 3 - 4 hours
10. Turn heat to high, add the fresh or frozen corn kernels, and cook for another 1/2 hour
11. Stir in the cilantro or scallions
12. Salt and pepper to taste

Zucchini Cashew Soup - Coach Tammy

You know that friend who's had babies but whose belly looks like she's never stopped doing crunches for even a second? No? Me neither. Until I met Tammy, that is. She has the very definition of washboard abs. When I asked her secret, she said, "Abs are made in the kitchen, not in the gym," and handed me a stack of her go-to recipes. This one is my favorite. There's something so simple and nourishing about it. As a bonus, it leads to a healthy and strong body. Thanks, Tam-tastic!

You will need:
- 1 medium zucchini, cleaned and chopped
- 1 cup of raw unsalted cashews rinsed
- 3½ cups vegetable stock

Directions:
1. In a medium saucepan, combine all ingredients and simmer over medium heat until the cashews are soft and break crumble easily.
2. Remove from heat and pour into blender (be careful not to burn yourself. Covering your blender with a towel while processing can help).
3. Blend until smooth.

He gives food to every creature. His love endures forever.
Psalms 136:25

Soft Cashew Cheese

You will need:

10 oz raw cashews

½ cup water

Juice of ½ lemon

½ cup parsley

1 tablespoon dill

1 teaspoon basil

1 teaspoon pepper

1 teaspoon dried garlic

1 teaspoon dried onion

¼ teaspoon salt

Directions:
1. Put cashew in food processor and pulse until ground.
2. Add water and pulse until creamy.
3. Add remaining ingredients and pulse until smooth.

Serve with flax bread, toast, or veggies.

Giant Batch of Hummus - Great Grandma Nora

You will need:

1 lb. can of chickpeas

1/3 cup tahini

Juice of 1 or 2 lemons

1 clove of garlic (more to taste)

Salt to taste

3 Tablespoons of olive oil

Directions:
1. Boil chickpeas in liquid from the can for 5 minutes on medium heat.
2. Drain.
3. Place chickpeas, tahini, lemon juice, garlic, and salt in blender.
4. Blend for about 15 seconds to make a smooth paste.

Look at how clean this recipe is. It needs no adaptation, but if you want, you can drain and rinse the chickpeas and even skip the boiling step. Grandma boiled them, but you don't have to. Just make sure to rinse them well. If you want to go super traditional, you can grow your own chickpeas like a hero or start with dried ones. Organic is always best, but get what you can and enjoy it to the max!

Consider using hummus as a sandwich spread, a dip, or added to soup and salad.

Homemade Yogurt – Grandma Mary (Adapted)

Pressure cookers have always scared me, with stories circulating through our family history about explosions and spaghetti sauce on the ceiling. However, when all of America erupted with blog after blog and photo after photo of happy, healthy mamas smiling next to their shiny little cooker-pots...I BIT!

By now, I'm sure you've heard that probiotics are a blessing for your belly, digestion, and entire system. They are healing ninjas! I want an army of them!

Mostly, I wanted to be able to push a button that says "Yogurt" and then watch a tiny little miracle happen. And THAT'S exactly what I feel has happened.

My Syrian grandma, Mary, used to make her own yogurt and...Holy EASY Batman! So... if you are feeling adventurous or just want to up that pro-biotic count, this is for you. I don't know about you, but if I'm using something called the "Instant Pot," it better be easy; this recipe doesn't disappoint.

You will need:
2 cans organic coconut cream
2 tablespoons real maple syrup
4 caps probiotics
1½ teaspoon gelatin
2 ball jars

Directions:
1. Mix coconut cream, maple syrup, and probiotics.
2. Split between your two clean ball jars.
3. Place uncovered in your Instant Pot for 11 hours.
4. When your little pot sings its happy "I'm done" song, it will read "Yogurt" on the display!

5. Pull out the jars
6. Stir in gelatin (or better yet, BLEND)
7. Please place them in refrigerator until they are cool.

And they're SO cool! I hope you enjoy this, and thanks to the blogger at My Big Fat Grain Free Life for starting this idea (note that she doesn't add syrup, so hers is pure plain yogurt, while this one is a tiny bit sweet).

Top with your favorites: Berries....MORE syrup? Have fun, sweet ones! Live large with little!

8 Curries, Lentils, & Beans

"And you, take wheat and barley, beans and lentils, millet and emmer, and put them into a single vessel and make your bread from them. During the number of days that you lie on your side, 390 days, you shall eat it.

Ezekiel 4:9

Curried Veggies

You will need:

1/2 onion, diced

3 cloves garlic, diced

2 tablespoon vegan butter or oil

1/2 cup yellow curry paste

1½ cup veggie broth

2 potatoes, cubed

4 medium carrots, cubed

1 package tempeh, cubed

1 can coconut milk

1/4 teaspoon cinnamon

1 tablespoon Siracha

1/4 teaspoon ground mustard

1/2 bag frozen peas

Directions:
1. Add onion, garlic, butter/oil, curry paste, veggie broth, potato, carrot, cinnamon, Siracha, and ground mustard to a crock pot on high.
2. Set the crock pot for 4 hours and sit back and wait.
3. About a half hour before the time is up, add coconut milk and frozen peas. The sauce will thicken and the peas will warm through, but be sure not to overcook the them!

Serve over rice.

Mujadara "Lentils with Rice" – Great Grandma Nora

You will need:

1 cup lentils

1/3 cup rice

2 large onions

3 cups of water

1 teaspoon cumin

¼ cup oil

Salt and pepper to taste

Directions:
1. Combine lentils, water, salt, and pepper.
2. Cook over medium heat for 7 minutes or until lentils are half cooked.
3. Add rice and cumin powder.
4. Cook until water is absorbed and rice is tender.
5. Quarter and slice peeled onions.
6. Fry the onions in oil until they are dark brown.
7. Drain the onions and place them to the side.
8. Pour the cooked oil over the Mujadara.
9. Mix well.
10. Garnish with onions.

Serve with a finely chopped cucumber and tomato salad and/or yogurt.

Jacque's Baked Beans – Mom (adapted)

From my half-Irish mom, Boston Baked Beans are like candy and great for potlucks. Vegans (and pigs) will appreciate this pork-free spin on Mom's original recipe, which includes ¼ pound of salt pork. This is a crockpot dish.

You will need:

1 lb. navy beans

2 tablespoons brown sugar (substitute with coconut sugar, monk fruit, maple syrup or molasses)

1 teaspoon tomato paste

1 teaspoon sesame oil

1 teaspoon mustard powder

2 teaspoons salt

¼ teaspoon pepper

3 tablespoons catsup (find this recipe on page 83)

4 cups water

Directions:
1. Wash beans and soak them for at least an hour in warm water.
2. Place beans, water, seasonings and salt pork in crock pot.
3. Stir and cover.
4. Bake on low 8-10 hours.

9 Noodles, Rice, Breads & Crusts

Better is a dry morsel and quietness with it
Than a house full of feasting with strife.

Proverbs 17:1

Noodles

One Egg Noodles – Grandma Kay

I was once shown this by my grandma when I was little and once again by my Father in Heaven when I was hungry.

These are approximate measurements and an approximate recipe. When I first made it, I used water because I didn't have any milk. You can make this smaller if you have less flour. You'll feel the firm resistance of the dough and know.

It's gonna' be good!

You will need:
1 egg
1/8-1/4 cup unsweetened nut milk or water
1 cup spelt, einkorn flour, or flour of choice
1 teaspoon salt
½ teaspoon baking soda (optional for fluffy noodles)

Directions for Making the Dough:
1. Flour your countertop.
2. In a large glass bowl, mix together dry ingredients.
3. Make a "well" in the center of your flour large enough to hold your egg.
4. Crack your egg in the center of your well.
5. Use a fork to scramble the egg gently.
6. Slowly fold the flour into the egg, adding the liquid of choice in very small amounts until a firm dough forms. It should feel between cookie dough and bread dough.
7. Form dough into a ball and transfer it to your floured counter.

8. Knead the dough until it feels smooth and incorporated (this is the part when Grandma says you put the love in).
9. Roll the dough into a log shape and rest for 10-20 minutes.
10. Cut ¼ inch slices.
11. Roll out each slice.

Directions for Making the Noodles:
1. Cut dough into strips using a knife or pizza cutter (unless you're blessed with a noodle maker, then go crazy).
    Tip: Roll on floured wax paper for easy cleanup when rolling out the dough!
2. Spread noodles out, dusting with a flour.
3. Let sit for 10 minutes. Note: the noodles will double in size once cooked so always try to cut them thin (unless you want chunky noodles).
4. Add noodles to boiling water and boil for 8-10 minutes. When they float, they are ready.

Top with butter or non-dairy butter, olive oil, and Garlic Powder. Add the sauce of your choice, vegan parm, and fresh herbs of your choice.

The leftover noodles are great pan-fried. You can also freeze them for a great gift, easy dinner, or snack.

Breads

Jesus said to them, "I am the bread of life; the one who comes to Me will not be hungry, and the one who believes in Me will never be thirsty.

John 6:35

In medieval times, community bread ovens were a central part of village life. A large communal brick oven would be built in the center of town, allowing villagers to gather once or twice a week to bake their bread together, sharing the heat and often the stories and news of the day while waiting for their loaves to bake. Each family would score the tops of their loaves with a knife to signify each loaf's home. Sometimes a simple cross or star was used, but often initials or more intricate vines and flowers set the loaves apart.

Easy Irish Spelt Soda Bread – Great Grandma Kay

How do those church ladies do it with their amazing fresh bread? Turns out, it can be a breeze.

You will need:
2 and 1/3 cup spelt flour, plus extra for dusting
2 teaspoon baking powder (aluminum free)
Salt
1 cup plain coconut, vanilla, or cashew yoghurt

Directions:
1. Preheat the oven to 425.
2. Place a baking stone or tray inside the oven to heat up.
3. In a large bowl, stir together all dry ingredients.
4. Add the yoghurt and stir until combined to a sticky dough.
5. Transfer the dough onto a lightly floured surface and shape it round with your hands.
6. Dust with flour then mark a deep cross on the top.
7. Transfer your loaf to the pre-heated baking tray or stone and bake for 15 - 20 minutes until crusty and golden and the bottom sounds hollow when tapped.
8. Allow it to cool completely before slicing. Can also be sliced and frozen.

Amazing when served with soup, salad, or just a jar of peanut butter.

Gluten Free White Sandwich Bread

You will need:

Dry Ingredients:

- 3 cups high quality gluten-free all-purpose flour containing xanthan gum
  - *I've only tested this recipe with King Arthur's Measure for Measure*
- ½ tbsp. Xanthan gum
- 1 packet of instant rapid rise yeast
- 1 teaspoon baking powder
- 1 teaspoon salt

Wet Ingredients:

- 1 ½ cups water warmed to 110° F.
- 2 large eggs room temperature
- ¼ cup honey
- ¼ cup vegetable oil

Instructions

1. Prepare a 9x5 loaf pan by greasing the bottom and halfway up the sides with butter or cooking spray.
2. Using the bowl of a stand mixer with the paddle attachment or large bowl, combine the dry ingredients (GF flour, yeast, Xanthan gum, baking powder, and salt.) *I use a handheld electric mixer.*
3. Add in wet ingredients (eggs, vegetable oil, honey, and warm water.) Mix on low until just combined. Turn the speed to medium and mix for 5 minutes, scraping down the bowl occasionally. This helps air bubbles get into the dough, making for a soft crumb. The batter should be a little thicker than the consistency of cake batter.
4. Pour the bread batter into the prepared loaf pan. Use a silicone spatula to Smoothen the top of the bread until it is even.
5. Cover the loaf pan in plastic wrap. *Tip: You can spray the underside of the plastic wrap with cooking spray to prevent sticking.*
6. Set the loaf pan in a warm place to rise for 45-60 minutes.
7. Around the 40-minute mark, preheat the oven to 350 F. Position a rack in the center of the oven.
8. Remove plastic wrap and bake the bread for a total of 40-45 minutes, until the bread's internal temperature reads 205 degrees. Around the halfway mark once the bread is golden, tent a piece of foil loosely around the top to stop it from browning.
9. Remove the bread from the oven and allow it to cool for about 5 minutes in the pan before removing it to a wire cooling rack.
10. Cool the bread completely, about 3 hours, before slicing with a bread knife.

Arabic Bread – Grandma Mary/Grandma Nora and her mom before that.

As a kid, I didn't know sandwich bread existed. Grandma Mary faithfully shared heaps and mountains of "Syrian Bread" to the point that it obliterated all other bread from existence. Syrian bread, stuffed with tabouli, toasted, dripping with butter, and packed with melting peanut butter, gives the feeling of down-home love that I imagine someone from Georgia feels when they think of biscuits. This recipe is adapted to be a much smaller batch; Grandma's recipe calls for 5 lbs. of flour! This recipe is shared as she shared it with me, but I am also adding substitutions so you can make this without the wheat flour.

You will need:
3 1/3 cups flour (substitute with spelt or einkorn flour)
1 envelope dry yeast
1 2/3 cups lukewarm water (approximate)
2/3 tablespoon salt
1/6 teaspoon raw sugar (or coconut sugar)

Directions:
1. Dissolve yeast in water.
2. Sprinkle with sugar.
3. Cover and let rise.
4. In a large pan, mix flour and salt.
5. Add yeast mixture.
6. Gradually add the lukewarm water, mixing and kneading until dough is smooth (this dough must be firm enough to roll with a rolling pin).
7. Cover with a towel or put in a warm place for 1-2 hours, or until dough rises.
8. Cut dough into sections the size of an orange (to make buns) or grapefruit (to make a small loaf).
9. Form into balls to make them round and smooth.
10. Let rest for 30 minutes under blankets.
11. Bake at 350 in a preheated oven for about 15 minutes or until golden brown.
12. Baste with oil, egg or melted vegan butter.

This is the same bread that is rolled flat and filled with meats or vegetables, then baked. It is known as Sfeeha or Meat Pies.

Sfeeha (Read Swvee-haa) – Grandma Mary

Welcome to my favorite food. This is the bite to beat all other bites. It is ancient food that was surely made for hundreds of years on community ovens and small outdoor fires. It is my soul food. It is the Syrian answer to pizza or quesadilla. This is Sfeeha.

You will need:
1 lb. diced mushrooms
1 onion, chopped
¼ cup pine nuts (or whatever you happen to have)
Juice of ½ a lemon or splash of vinegar (red wine or whatever you happen to have)
Salt, pepper, and allspice to taste
¼ cup olive oil or vegan butter
Pastry dough (learn how to make this on page 130)

Directions:
1. Preheat oven to 400 degrees
2. Sauté onions in vegan butter or olive oil.
3. Add meat (or mushrooms) and spices.
4. Sauté until tender.
5. Add nuts and brown them.
6. Add lemon or vinegar.
7. Mix well.
8. Place on raw dough, spread close to the edges and tuck edges in.
9. Pinch them to close or serve open-faced.
10. Place on a greased baking sheet.
11. Bake in oven until meat and dough are lightly browned.

Sesame Sunflower Flax Bread – Inspired by Detroit Zen Center Raw Food Kitchen

My daughter LOVES this. My friend said I was trying to kill her when she tried it. No offense taken. Is it an acquired taste?

You will need:
1 cup ground flax seeds
1/3 cup whole flax
2/3 cup sunflower seeds
¼ cup sesame seeds
½ teaspoon sea salt
1 clove garlic minced
2 tablespoons onion chopped
1 1/3 cup water

Directions:
1. Mix ground and whole flax, salt, garlic, onion, and water.
2. Add sunflower and sesame seeds and mix well.
3. Use the back of a spoon to spread the batter evenly on a dehydrator tray.
4. Dry at 105 for 4 hours.
5. Flip and score into 9 slices (or more).
6. Dehydrate another hour (or longer if you want crispy bread).

This bread keeps soft in the refrigerator for two weeks. If you dry them to a cracker crisp, they will last longer!

Crusts

My mom was named Jacque. She was an AMAZING cook—so good that when she was a Junior in High School, she won a trip to Washington, D.C., for making the best pasties in the U.P. (Michigan's Upper Peninsula).

That's a huge achievement since almost all pasties originate from the U.P. They were a daily lunchbox staple for the men working in the mines, including my great-grandpa.

This recipe is a family secret, and I have thought deeply about sharing it with you. Promise me you won't start a business selling this pasty, because I dream of doing that one day. "Jacque's Pasties" has a nice ring to it, don't you think? I'm going to share, and here's why.

When my mom and dad died in a tornado, there was almost nothing left behind. However, we did find several kitchen items from Mom. As I pulled them from the debris, I felt as if my mom were saying to me, "This is how you will keep us alive. Set the table, prepare the food, and when you do, share the story of who we were."

So, here's who she was: She was the type of woman who arrived in D.C. on that trip as a social justice activist. Her first stop was the Lincoln Memorial, where a KKK protest was taking place.

At 16 years old, she boldly approached the Klan and exclaimed, "How dare you? Don't you know it was Lincoln who freed the slaves?" They responded, "And we have the hard-earned right to protest anywhere we want. This is public land."

That's the story she always told as she baked these perfect pasties. So, as you make and enjoy them, thanks be to my mom for the inspiration in so very many ways.

Pasty Crust – Mom

You will need:

3 cups flour (Mom used white and I use spelt)

1½ teaspoons salt

3/4 teaspoon baking powder (aluminum free)

1 cup shortening or 1 cup lard

3/4 or 2 cups coconut oil

1 cup ice water

1 tablespoon of white vinegar

Directions:
1. Mix dry ingredients in mixing bowl.
2. Cut in shortening until the mixture resembles coarse crumbs.
3. Add ice water a little at a time, tossing with a fork to make a pastry-like dough.
4. Add a bit more water and the vinegar until the dough holds together.
5. Roll dough out on a lightly floured surface (or on top of a piece of plastic wrap which can easily be folded over and then peeled off once the pasty ingredients are loaded).
6. Brush edges of pasty with a smidgen of water.
7. Crimp very firmly with a fork twice.
8. Brush tops of finished pasties with egg.

Note: Like pastry dough, pasty dough should be handled as little as possible to ensure flakiness. So, handle with care!

FAMILY SECRET ALERT!
When you roll this dough out, use a pie tin as your guide. Place the rolled dough in the pie tin and fill half with the filling. Then, fold over, crimp the edges, and move the pie to a cookie sheet!

Pasty Filling – Mom

For a veggie pasty,
You will need:
1 cleaned and chopped cauliflower
1 cleaned and chopped head of broccoli
3 peeled and chopped carrots
2 large potatoes, diced
1/2 large yellow onion, diced
salt
pepper

For Mom's Original Recipe, you will need:
1 package of ground chuck (use meat of choice or pack with broccoli and cauliflower or your favorites).
2 large potatoes, diced
1/2 a large yellow onion diced
1 rutabaga, diced
salt
pepper

Directions:
1. Fill the crust (page 130) with raw ingredients and bake at 400 degrees for about 40 minutes.
2. Served with homemade catsup (page 83).

P.S.
My Great Grandma Kay's last words were: "Pasties. Pasties for all the men."

I amazing how every culture makes something like my Great Grandma's pasties. Empanada, sopapia, calzone, pasty. Gimme!

Nut Crust

You will need:

1½ cups pecan meal (finely crushed pecans)

¼ cups vanilla stevia to taste

1½ teaspoon cinnamon

6 tablespoons unsalted vegan butter, melted

1 large egg, lightly beaten

1 teaspoon vanilla

Directions:
1. Preheat oven to 325 degrees.
2. Combine pecan meal, stevia, and cinnamon.
3. Stir in melted butter, egg and vanilla; combine well.
4. Press into and up the sides of a 10-inch pie pan.
5. Set it aside.
6. Pour filling of choice into the crust.
7. Bake for about 50 minutes or until filling is nearly firm in center.
8. Cool completely.
9. Refrigerate before serving.

10 Desserts

My son, eat honey, for it is good;
Yes, the honey from the comb is sweet to your taste

Proverbs 24:13

My family tree has an overabundance of Diabetes: my mom, aunty, grandma, and even great grandma were (are) all Diabetic.

Not this girl!

Years ago, I was blessed to have a massage (I know, swoon) and at the end of the massage, I asked the therapist if he noticed anything that was out of line.

"Nope" he said, "All the bones and muscles are in right order, but you eat too much sugar, that's why your back hurts RIGHT THERE" as he pressed into the spot on the right side of my middle back that ALWAYS hurt.

"What? What do you mean?" With a shrug of his shoulder, he gave me insight that would change everything.

"That's not a muscle hurting," he explained. That's where your pancreas is. It's inflamed. Don't believe me? Cut out refined sugar for a week and see if you notice a difference." He further explained that I didn't even have to cut out all sugar, just the white stuff. I could switch to raw sugar or honey.

I did. And guess what! No. More. Back pain!

So, let's begin there. If you experience pain in the right side of your middle back, eliminate white sugar for a week and observe if anything changes. Let's reclaim the health God bestowed upon us, one step, bite, and choice at a time. And let's create delicious food!

Flourless Chocolate Cake

I've spun this recipe a million ways.

When I auditioned for the Great American Baking Show, this was my audition piece, displayed as a single. I called it Flourless Chocolate Cake, and they called it "moist" and "one of the tastiest bites of the day."

When I divorced my ex, I had a divorce party. The cake I made for that was a layered cake. I filled it with fresh raspberries and topped it with cherry glaze. Like the divorce, it was dark, delicious, and healthy.

On a regular basis, this just gets poured into a 9X13 baking pan and served as brownies.

You. Can't. Loose.

This recipe will yield 10-12 servings.

You will need:
1 15.5 oz. can black beans, thoroughly rinsed and drained
1/2 teaspoon baking powder
1/2 cup + 1 tablespoon sugar or Xylitol
1/4 cup dark cocoa powder
3 eggs
3 tablespoons olive oil
1 teaspoon vanilla
1 teaspoon instant coffee granule or 1 shot of espresso
1/4 cup walnuts, chopped, optional
1/3 cup Lilly's chocolate chips (or similar)

Directions:
1. Preheat oven to 350 degrees.
2. Place parchment paper in the bottom of an 8x8 pan.
3. Grease the parchment paper. This will be your security blanket to ensure the brownies don't stick to the pan!!
4. Place all ingredients except chocolate chips and walnuts in a food processor or blender.
5. Pulse thoroughly until smooth and well combined.
6. Pour batter in the baking dish.
7. Top with nuts and chocolate chips.
8. Bake for 30-35 minutes or until the top is dry and edges begin to pull away from the baking dish.
9. Cool completely before cutting.

Grandma's Company Coffee Cake – Grandma Kathy

My grandma, Kathy, was an amazing woman. She left our tiny hometown to study Nursing in Detroit. When she returned, she became the Director of Nursing for the 18-bed hospital. She was a working woman, a great leader, and an example I strove to follow. However, she was not a great cook. This was one of her wins. She would make it on weekends, and when she did, I came running.

You will need:

1 stick of oleo (or unsalted non-dairy butter)

1½ cups sugar (or monk fruit, xylitol, or coconut sugar)

3 eggs

½ pint sour cream (or non-dairy plain yogurt)

1 teaspoon vanilla extract

2 cups flour (or spelt, einkorn, etc.)

1 teaspoon baking powder

1 teaspoon baking soda

1 teaspoon salt

1 cup nuts of choice

1 teaspoon cinnamon

Directions:
1. Cream together 1 stick of oleo, 1 cup of sugar, and 3 eggs.
2. Mix in sour cream and vanilla extract.
3. Sift or whisk together flour, baking powder, baking soda, and salt.
4. Add the wet to the dry and incorporate until smooth.
5. Pour ½ mixture into greased Bundt pan.
6. Mix most chopped nuts, ½ cup sugar, and cinnamon.
7. Swirl with knife.
8. Add remaining batter.
9. Sprinkle remainder of the nut mixture over the top.
10. Bake at 350 for 45-50 minutes.

Gluten Free White Cake – Found on a Rice Flour Package

This recipe flew right under the radar of my mother-in-law. She didn't remark that it "tasted funny" or ask, "Is this health food?" And believe me, she would have. If she can't tell, neither will your pickiest eater.

You will need:

1½ cups all-purpose gluten free flour

1 cup of granulated sweetener of choice

2 teaspoons baking powder

1/3 teaspoon baking soda

½ teaspoon salt

2 eggs (for yellow cake) or 4 egg whites for white cake

½ cup mild flavored oil (melted coconut, extra virgin olive oil, etc.)

1 tablespoon white vinegar

1 teaspoon extract of choice (vanilla, coconut, etc.)

½ cup of non-dairy milk of choice

For Chocolate Cake, add ¼ cup cocoa and ¼ cup additional milk.

Directions:
1. Preheat Oven to 350 degrees.
2. Oil one 8- or 9-inch round pan or line 12 muffin cup pan with cupcake paper.
3. Bring all ingredients to room temperature.
4. Sift the dry ingredients together in a bowl.
5. In a separate mixing bowl, combine the liquid ingredients, except the milk.
6. Slowly pour dry mix into the liquids and begin to stir, adding the milk while stirring to keep the flour from flying up and out of the bowl while mixing.
7. Continue to beat at medium speed just until the lumps are gone, and the batter is smooth.
8. Pour batter into prepared pan(s). Allow it to rest in pan for 15 minutes.

9. Bake for approximately 30-35 minutes for cake and 20-25 minutes for cupcakes.
10. Test with a toothpick before removing the cake from the oven. When done, the toothpick should come out clean (not wet) and may have a few crumbs attached when inserted into the center of the cake. Glass, metal, and ceramic pans all alter the baking time, so check for doneness before removing the cake from the oven.
11. Remove from oven to cool on a wire rack.
12. To remove the cake, gently invert the cake by flipping it upside down onto your hand, removing the pan, then returning the cake to the wire rack or serving plate.

This cake can be stacked like a Victoria Sponge Cake, with jam between the layers.

Chia Jam

Last night, I checked the price of a jar of jam. It was almost $6. My stars! Peanut butter and jelly is the budget-stretching staple for most American families. How do we keep those PB&Js coming for our kiddos, packed with nutrition but easy on the pocketbook? Make that jam! Chia is such a wonderful seed; it packs 5g of protein and 10g of fiber in each 1 oz serving. Plus, it is full of omega-3s and gels, making it perfect for jams and puddings.

You will need:
2 cups of berries (pick your favorite!)
½ cup agave
¾ cup chia seeds
Vanilla or stevia extract (optional)

Directions:
1. Blend together berries and agave.
2. Pour into a saucepan over medium-low heat.
3. Stir in ¾ cup of chia seeds.
4. Stir until thickened (about 15 minutes).

5. Add ½ dropper vanilla stevia or vanilla extract (optional).
6. Pour into a sterile jar and can or pour into any storage (like a glass bowl etc.) and keep in the fridge.

Raw Vegan Cupcakes – My former coworker, Holly

There's a joke:
Question: How do you tell who's Vegan at the party?
Answer: Don't worry. They'll tell YOU.
So true.
Holly was the most Vegan-Vegan I've ever met.
She made these for me on a very long and stressful work trip and they saved the day, so I saved the recipe!
Here's what my kids said:

Liam (age 9): MMMMM...this is the best cupcake ever!
Alex (age 16): Not bad! Good!

You will need:
2 cups raw walnuts
1 cup raw unsweetened coconut, shredded
1/2 cup any raw nut butter
1/2 cup agave or maple syrup

Directions:
1. Process all ingredients in a food processor until it's "dough-like"
2. Form into sprayed muffin pan and refrigerate.

It's that easy!

Raw Vegan Frosting – Holly

You will need:

½ cup raw unsweetened coconut flakes (soak to rehydrate)

¼ cup maple syrup

½ teaspoon vanilla extract or 1 scoop vanilla protein powder

Directions:
1. Blend all ingredients until smooth.
2. Pour into a storage or piping bag.
3. Refrigerate.
4. Snip the corner of the bag and use it to frost cupcakes, cake, or anything else you desire!

Heavens to Betsy Gluten-Free Carrot Cake

This classic carrot cake recipe has been tweaked a bit, removing refined sugar and replacing it with kinder, gentler sugars. I hope you love it!

You will need:
12 oz carrots, peeled and tops removed
½ cup of finely chopped walnuts
5 large eggs
1 teaspoon baking powder
½ teaspoon baking soda
9 oz almond meal
1 cup maple syrup
1 teaspoon ground cinnamon
¼ teaspoon ground nutmeg
1 teaspoon of ground ginger

Directions:
1. Grease two 8-inch round cake pans and preheat the oven to 350 degrees.
2. Grate the carrots using a food processor.
3. Remove the grater attachment from the food processor and switch to the chopping attachment.
4. Add the walnuts and pulse until roughly chopped.
5. Set aside with the carrots.
6. Add the remaining cake ingredients (except the carrots and walnuts) and process to combine.
7. Finally, add the carrot and walnuts and pulse to combine them with the cake batter.
8. Divide the batter between the prepared springform pans and bake for 15 to 25 minutes.

9. Remove from the oven and let the cake cool completely in the tin before removing.

Cream Cheese Frosting

You will need:

8oz cream Neufchâtel, at room temperature (or other non-dairy cream cheese)

1/3 cup of coconut oil, at room temperature

½ cup agave

Zest and juice of half a lemon, or to taste

Directions:
1. Combine the coconut oil and Neufchatel in the bowl of an electric mixer.
2. Fit the mixer with a paddle attachment and beat until smooth and creamy.
3. Add the agave, lemon juice, and zest and beat for another 5 minutes, or until pale and fluffy.
4. Cool in fridge.
5. If you are using this frosting on a cake, spread the frosting between the cake layers and over the top of the cooled cake.

This was the BOMB! When I make it again, I will add one scoop of vanilla protein powder to this healthy treat!

The World's Cleanest Cookie

When I became a student of Traditional Naturopathic Medicine at Genesis School of Natural Health, I was interested to learn that the first phases of the program largely dealt with the issue of Cancer in the body.

There are plenty of reasons to be encouraged about how nutrition and lifestyle can reduce your cancer risks and reverse the progress of the disease. As naturopathic doctors collaborate with allopathic doctors, I am hopeful about the progress in overall wellness that can be achieved at little to no cost to individuals seeking health and healing. This holds true not only in the area of cancer. Hippocrates was literal when he said, "Let your food be your medicine." Real, organic, nutritious food can indeed be strong and powerful agents of healing.

The first book I studied while a student with Genesis was *The Gerson Therapy* by Charlotte Gerson and Morton Walker, D.P. M. This is the brainchild of Max Gerson, M.D., who, while a student, was looking for a way to help with his personal maladies. He landed on a dietary protocol that seems to be helpful at least and miraculous at best. If you have a loved one who is seeking to heal Cancer, this book is a must-read.

The therapy consists of a combination of cooked and juiced fruits and vegetables. You may find that following the Gerson diet results in a substantial amount of apple and carrot pulp. While some high-end juicers approved by The Gerson Institute leave very little pulp behind, let's be realistic. Many, if not most of us, are using more conventional juicers. This means that until one can invest in a higher-end juicer, they will, while following the Gerson Diet, accumulate a LOT of pulp. Composting is an obvious option, but it seems a bit wasteful when there is clearly so much life, health, and good ol' yumminess left in this pulp.

So, to make something good out of all that pulp, I created this little treat:

I'm referring to them as Gerson Therapy Cookies, although they are not endorsed by the Gerson Institute. While they are free from that undesirable white stuff, the sugar content is not really something anyone would recommend for someone with Cancer or any other illness. However, if you find yourself in a situation like mine, with a family member following the Gerson Therapy for healing and a bunch of leftover pulp, this may be suitable for you. The recipe is simple:

The World's Cleanest Cookie

You will need:
3 cups carrot, apple pulp (made from approximately 4 carrots, 2 red apples.)
3 eggs
¼ cup liquid coconut oil (can omit if desired)
¼ teaspoon vanilla extract
½ cup water
¼ cup real maple syrup
1 tablespoon black strap molasses
½ teaspoon vanilla liquid stevia
2½ tablespoon ground cinnamon (optional)
1 teaspoon ground cloves (optional)
½ teaspoon allspice (optional)
¾ teaspoon sea salt (optional)
2 teaspoons gluten free baking soda
¼ teaspoon baking powder
1/3 cup flax meal
2/3 cup organic oats
½ cup shredded coconut
½ cup chopped dried dates
½ cup chopped dried fruit (optional)

Directions:
1. Preheat your oven to 380 degrees.
2. In a food processor, place the juice pulp, dates, egg, olive oil, water, and chopped apple.
3. Turn the food processor on until the mixture is well incorporated and smooth.
4. Add the cinnamon, cloves, allspice, salt, vanilla liquid stevia, baking soda, baking powder, and flax.
5. Periodically, stop the food processor and scrape the bowl with a spatula.
6. Mix the batter until thoroughly incorporated. It will be very thick.
7. Once the batter is mixed, scoop it into a large mixing bowl.
8. Add the oats to the mixing bowl. You can also add chopped, dried fruit, if you want to. Incorporate the nuts, coconut, and dried fruit into the batter using a wooden spoon or spatula.
9. Liberally grease two mini muffin trays or cookie sheets (that contain 12 muffin molds, each) with coconut oil.
10. Mold each cookie, by hand: using a spoon, fill each mini muffin mold, halfway. Then, take a second scoop of cookie batter, and form it into a mound shape.
11. Use your hands to help you mold the cookies into muffin shapes.
12. Place the muffin trays into the preheated oven for 30-35 minutes.
13. Once baked, you want the cookies to be a deep brown color. After baking, cool the cookies on a baking rack. Let them completely cool before you sample them.

Notes:

Juice Pulp - You can freeze carrot and apple pulp in 3-cup portions. When you're ready to make cookies, just put the frozen juice pulp in a pan and bake it in the preheated oven. It will thaw in about 4-5 minutes.

Stevia - You can substitute 2 tablespoons of coconut sugar for the vanilla liquid stevia.

Storage - Do not store these cookies in a tightly sealed container. They are too moist. Just place them on a plate, covered loosely.

Gluten Free Short Bread Cookies

You will need:

¾ cup coconut flour

¾ cup white rice flour

½ teaspoon salt

1 cup coconut oil

½ cup powdered sweetener of your choice

Directions
1. Mix coconut flour, white rice flour, and salt in a bowl.
2. In another bowl, cream, coconut oil, and powdered sweetener together.
3. Mix together.
4. Once these are mixed into a ball (it will be a little crumbly and you have to work it a bit it holds it together, cut in two and roll the dough into two balls.
5. Refrigerate for 30 minutes while preheating your oven to 350.
6. Once the dough is chilled, roll into two "logs."
7. Roll the logs in powdered sugar and slice into even pieces.
8. Bake for 7-10 minutes. Do. Not. Allow them to brown.
9. Allow them to cool on the sheet for at least 10 minutes. If you try to pull them off early, they WILL crumble. So, patience, beloved.

These came out perfectly; even my gluten-loving friends loved them! Let me know if you give this a try! These are the BEST served with green tea and milk.

Vegan Magic Shell aka A Flight of Chocolate Tarts

Making your own dairy-free or vegan magic shell is probably one of the easiest things ever. It requires just three ingredients: coconut oil, cocoa powder, and a sweetener. You probably already have all these ingredients in stock in your gluten-free vegan pantry!

Coconut oil has the unique property of liquefying when warmed and solidifying when cooled. By making your own vegan magic shell, you're essentially getting the best of both worlds! You achieve that magical chocolatey shell you're looking for, but with control over the ingredients and the option to create a healthier recipe tailored to your diet (i.e. making it dairy-free, soy-free, refined sugar-free, gluten-free, raw, etc.).

You will need:
1 cup coconut oil, liquified
½ cup cocoa powder (or carob powder)
6 tablespoons liquid sweetener of your choice (I used maple syrup), room temperature
2 Teaspoons pure vanilla extract
Pinch of salt

Optional: Add 1-2 teaspoons tapioca starch for a thicker mixture (I only do this if I'm using it as a drizzle over cakes).

Directions:
1. Make sure your coconut oil is liquified, but not hot. If you need to heat it to melt it, then allow it some time to cool first.
2. Place all ingredients in a glass bowl (I use a tall measuring cup).
3. Mix with a spoon until all the ingredients are incorporated and the mixture is smooth. This can take a few minutes -- just keep stirring until there are no clumps left behind.

Notes:

This can be used immediately to dip frozen desserts, chilled treats, or to drizzle over your favorite desserts.

You can halve or even quarter this recipe if you only want a small amount of drizzle. I make it in the quantity outlined above because if you want to dip items like frozen treats in it, you need a bit more substance for coating. This way, I usually have leftovers, which I simply store in a glass jar in the fridge.

If you store this in the fridge, it will solidify, so when you want to use it again, just bring it back to room temperature (by leaving it out of the fridge overnight, microwaving, etc.). It melts back into a liquid state easily, so just give it a stir, and it's ready for use again.

You can easily enhance this recipe by incorporating mint or any other flavors you prefer.

I've also greased mini tart pans, poured this in, and then let it chill.

You can create as many chocolate tarts as you like. You can also make tiny chocolates by pouring this into silicone molds.

Playing with chocolate is a One Egg Noodles approved pastime. But be warned that this can get messy fast.

Almond Baked Donuts

You will need:

1 cup almond flour

3 tablespoons honey or maple syrup

2 large eggs

2 teaspoons vanilla extract

1/4 teaspoon baking soda

Directions:
1. Preheat your oven to 300 degrees.
2. Grease your donut pan and set aside.
3. In a medium mixing bowl, mix all of your ingredients until smooth.
4. Fill your donut pans with your mixture (I use a piping bag or Ziplock bag with the corner trimmer), filling each donut section 1/2 way.
5. Bake for 10-15 minutes, keeping an eye on them and taking them out as soon as your donuts are cooked; test them by inserting a skewer into the middle (it should come out clean). Be sure not to overcook them as they'll dry out!
6. Allow to cool before removing from the tins and eating as is or topping with whatever your heart desires (stay tuned for more recipes!)

These donuts, stored in an airtight container, will keep in the fridge or at room temperature for 3-4 days. If you live in a humid climate, I'd suggest keeping them in the fridge so that they last longer. However, they will keep fine at room temperature if it's not too hot!

Option: Pineapple Upside Down Donuts

Directions:
1. Prepare as directed above and end by placing a single pineapple ring on top of each donut.
2. These will take a couple of extra minutes because of the added moisture from the fruit.

Toppings: Glaze with powdered sugar, Chocolate Glaze, or peanut butter. Sprinkle with powdered sugar (or a powdered sugar alternative) or cinnamon sugar (or a sugar alternative).

-

This is also enjoyable for the kids and even a delightful party treat when you bake the donuts and let your guests select from a topping and glaze bar. Additionally, this same recipe can be made into donut holes with the proper pan and does nicely as a yellow layer cake substitution.

The women of St. Barbara's Church in Vulcan, Michigan publish a cookbook every year. This book, which contains notes from my mother, survived the tornado that took her home. Suffice to say, the recipes are a sturdy stock, made of things like "oleo and eagle brand."

It contained 5 recipes for "hot dish"

It was "make do with what ya' got, kind food" from miners and immigrants whose Christmas cookies bring out the best in us. Something about the Crisco smooths things over. When the ladies and their families bring the confections in tins to the church for the swap, the sugar in the air softens the blow of hurt from the year passing. The time your kid did this or that to mine, or your husband gave my husband the business at work - it all crumbles like...well, like cookies.

Everyone has their favorite.
My great Grandma K was a diabetic (a diagnosis which she rebuked and ignored); bonbons were her favorite. She kept a stash of them on the breezeway, and she must have trusted me because I saw her pull the tin and scarf a few of them several times a day at Christmas time. She always sent me a little wink in my direction and a bonbon to keep her secret.

Each year, I roll them up. Sure, I could make them in my sleep now; they're in my blood. It's funny how that happens, but in reality, it doesn't *just* happen. That's why each year I call my kids to the kitchen when it's time to make "Grandma's bonbons."
Funny, too, how someday I will be the "Grandma" behind the bonbons.
Life is too short to hold a grudge-or even a secret recipe.

Flavors are caught in time.
Suspended like baked meringues.
There's something about it the binds us together.

Part Three: The Healing Home

Then my people will live in a peaceful settlement,
In secure dwellings, and in undisturbed resting places;
Isaiah 32:18

11 Good Clean Living

Blessed are the pure in heart for they shall see God

Matthew 5:8

Elderberry Syrup: Treat and Medicine

I learned the recipe for elderberry syrup while studying Medical Herbalism at Genesis School of Natural Health.

It's tried and true.

No matter how many tools you collect in your naturopathic toolkit, there will always be a star during cold and flu season: Elderberry! So, what's all the fuss about? First: the elderberries themselves:

Elderberries (Sambucus nigra and Sambucus canadensis)

What we know: They've been around for a long time! Hippocrates, the "father" of modern medicine, wrote about it. So did Dioscorides, a Greek physician, pharmacologist, botanist, and author of *De Materia Medica*. In a 1650 medical text, "elder" was translated from Latin to English as the "medicine chest of the common people."

The berries themselves are extremely nutritious. They are rich in flavonoids (obviously...check out that color!), high in Vitamins C and A, as well as iron and potassium. Their antioxidant content is off the charts. As for the honey in the syrup, it boasts powerful antiviral properties in addition to a high 'yummy' factor!

To Make Elderberry Syrup, you will need:
2/3 cup dried elderberries
3½ cups pure water
2 tablespoons ginger root
1 cinnamon stick
½ teaspoon clove
1 cup raw, unfiltered, no additives honey

(Note: I use all organic ingredients. It is advisable not to mix toxins with medicinals).

Directions:
1. Pour water, elderberries, ginger, cinnamon and clove into medium saucepan and bring to boil.
2. Once boiling, cover and reduce heat.
3. Reduce the liquid by about half. It will take 25 to 45 minutes, but the time will vary, so just watch it closely.
4. Once the syrup is reduced by ½, remove it from the heat.
5. Cool slightly, then strain into a glass bowl.
6. When the liquid is cooled to lukewarm, add the honey and stir until it is incorporated.
7. Pour into a 16 oz jar. Your syrup will last several months in the refrigerator.

Dosage:
Adults: 1 tablespoon
Children: 1 teaspoon

Take daily as a preventive during cold and flu season. At first sign of a cold, the dose can be raised to as much as 1 tablespoon per hour for adults and 1 Teaspoon per hour for children[1].

Here's some more good news! Elderberry syrup is so tasty that it's one medicine you won't have a fight get into happy, healthy tummies. You can also enjoy this as a mixer with spirits or with fizzy water!

---

[1] Infants under one year old should not ingest honey, as their digestive systems are not yet sufficiently developed.

Homemade Laundry Soap

Oh. My. Lanta. They want $18 for a bottle of laundry detergent! What would Grandma do? I feel like we know the answer. She'd make it, of course. I'm not Grandma, but this is how I make my homemade soap.

You will need:
½ cup washing soda
¼ cup borax
1 cup water
1 tablespoon castile (Dr. Brohner's Soap)
¼ cup white vinegar
Essential oil of your choosing

Directions:
1. Whisk washing soda with borax.
2. Add boiling water.
3. Stir in castile (a.k.a. Dr. Brohner's Soap).
4. Add white vinegar.
5. Add 20 drops of essential oil (lemon, lavender, jasmine…you decide).
6. Pour into an empty and clean gallon jug and top with hot water!
7. Cover and Shake.

BOOM! Mom Won!

1/4 Cup takes care of 1 large load!
Note: To make Washing Soda: Cover a cookie sheet with baking soda and bake for 20 minutes at 400 degrees.

Bath & Body Oil

You will need:

½ cup fractionated coconut oil

½ cup avocado oil

¼ cup olive oil

20 drops essential oil of your choice.

Directions:
1. Combine all ingredients in a measuring cup or bottle.
2. Stir or shake to combine.
3. Pour into an 8 oz. bottle or two 4 oz. bottles.

Apply to your body after showering or add a small amount to a hot bath. This can also be used as a massage oil.

If you want to make two different scents, pour the mixture into two 4 oz. bottles, and add 10 drops of essential oil to each bottle. Shake well to distribute the essential oils. There are many combinations of essential oils you can use for this summer bath and body oil. Here are a few of my favorites:

Peppermint: Great for a cooling experience after being out in the sun. Can sting. Don't get it near your eyes!

Lavendar: Good to help you calm down and sleep at night. A blind test in a nursing home in 1992 showed one drop of lavender helped guests sleep better than sleeping medication.

Lemon: Refreshing

Jasmine: Creativity

Eucalyptus: Clean sinuses. You can make mini-Fizzies to put them in the shower and help clear your head in cold and flu season (see page 163)!

Simple Sugar/Salt Scrub

Sugar and salt scrubs are super simple to make. You can hardly mess them up, and if you do, you can always fix them. Therefore, if you're feeling a bit hesitant with DIY, they're the ideal product to begin with.

Sugar scrubs can be made in seconds using ingredients you already have on hand. There is no need for specialty ingredients or tools. Just stir together sugar and oil, and boom! You've made an awesome sugar scrub.

This simple sugar scrub recipe leaves your skin soft and silky after just one use. With several applications, your skin will become more supple and moisturized.

This easy sugar scrub recipe requires just two ingredients. You can customize it however you like. The instructions below provide ideas for customizing the basic recipe.

Whip this up for an easy, all-natural way to exfoliate and soften your skin. This recipe also makes a fun girl's night project, or an easy and inexpensive sleepover craft for teens and tweens. Follow this ultra-easy recipe to get a swoon-worthy, professional-quality body polish—no cosmetic or chemistry PhD needed.

You will need:
1 cup granulated white sugar or salt.
½ cup vegetable oil (such as olive oil, coconut oil, avocado oil, or whatever you have)

Optional Ingredients for Customizing:

25 drops essential oil.

1 teaspoon dried herbs or dried flower petals.

2 to 5 drops food coloring in your choice of color.

Supplies:

Small mixing bowl

Silicone spatula or mixing spoon

Measuring cups

Jars or containers to package your scrubs

Directions:
1. Place sugar/salt into a bowl. Add in 1/3 cup of oil and stir until well blended.
2. If the sugar scrub seems too dry for your liking add more oil, 1 tablespoon at a time, until you get the consistency you like. Remember, this is personal preference so don't worry about "messing up." You won't, I promise.

If you'd like to dress up your scrub, you can add optional ingredients at this step. This is completely up to you, though; the scrub is lovely as-is.

3. Stir in essential oils of your choice for scent.
4. Mix in dried herbs or dried flower petals (they must be dried, not fresh).
5. Add cocoa powder, dry clay, or ground coffee beans—1 teaspoon measurement for each.
6. Stir in 2 to 5 drops of food coloring (you can add a few extra drops to get the color you're looking for).
7. Package your scrub in mason jars and upcycled jelly jars.

How To Use: Massage over the entire body in the bath or shower, using circular motions. Rinse well with warm water.

Homemade Bath Fizzies

You will need:

8 ounces baking soda

4 ounces cream of tartar

4 ounces cornstarch

4 ounces Epsom salts

¾ teaspoon distilled water

20-30 drops lavender essential oil - or your favorite essential oil

2 teaspoons coconut oil

Soap colorant - or food coloring, optional

Dried lavender (powder or flowers) - or biodegradable glitter or other decorative items

Directions:
1. In a large mixing bowl, mix together all the dry ingredients: Epsom salts, baking soda, corn starch, and cream of tartar.
2. Combine the water, oil, and food coloring in another small mixing bowl.
3. Combine the wet and dry ingredients. At this stage, your mixture should resemble wet sand. If you're using natural food coloring, you should be able to tell when it's well mixed once the coloring is even. It should also hold together when you squeeze some in your fist. If it doesn't, add a few drops of water at a time until you reach the desired consistency.
4. Once it's the right consistency, tightly pack it down into your mold (ice cube tray, mini muffin pan, etc.).
5. Allow the bath fizz to dry for 24 hours. I recommend not removing the mold until the mixture is completely dry. However, depending on your mold shape, you may have success with early removal so you can reuse the mold more quickly. Cupcake and flat shapes are great for removing them from the mold early. More intricate designs do not.

Once you're ready, remove your DIY bath bombs from the mold and store them in an airtight container.

To enjoy your bath fizz, simply drop one into the bathtub and experience the soothing aromatherapy.

Thick and Creamy Body Butter Recipe

Whatever your experience, in cold months, we're all looking for a solution to ease the discomfort of dry skin and restore it to its soft, silky form. Various over-the-counter solutions are available, but making your own ultra-moisturizing Creamy Body Butter is so easy!

This recipe contains simple ingredients that will leave your skin feeling soft, silky, and hydrated, even in the coldest months. It comes together quickly and is sure to be a favorite!

You will need:
1 cup shea butter
½ cup coconut oil
1 tablespoon Vitamin E oil (optional)
½ cup sweet almond oil
Storage Jar

Another option to enhance your body butter is to add fragrance. While this isn't necessary, as the body butter is wonderful on its own, incorporating a bit of fragrance oil or essential oil will leave your skin smelling as delightful as it feels. You can choose any scent that appeals to you!

Directions:
1. Combine shea butter, coconut oil, and sweet almond oil in a heat-safe bowl.
2. Place the bowl over a double boiler or similar set up.
3. Heat the ingredients slowly over medium-low heat.
4. Stirring occasionally, the mixture will slowly melt together. The mixture is done when all traces of individual ingredients (lumps of coconut oil or shea butter) have dissolved.
5. Carefully remove the bowl from the heat and allow to cool slightly (10 minutes).
6. If desired, stir in fragrance oil. I use 2 teaspoons of the Warm Vanilla Sugar fragrance oil for a lightly scented lotion. If you're planning on adding in a little vitamin E oil, you would do that at this time as well.
7. Place the bowl in the freezer for 15 to 20 minutes. The mixture should begin to solidify, but not be completely frozen.
8. Using an electric mixer (or hand mixer), whip the chilled mixture until light and fluffy. Don't worry, it will fluff right up!
9. Scoop the creamy body butter into jars with sealable lids!

Wasn't that easy? It's incredibly simple to create products at home that compete with store-bought items. Plus, you know exactly what ingredients are in your products! No harsh or harmful chemicals here!

Castor Oil

Castor Oil is a vegetable oil created from the Castor seed. It's first use was documented in an Egyptian tomb. Historians guess on the date with a range of 4,000-500 B.C.E. It was used cosmetically and medicinally. It's a natural laxative. It is prioritized in hair care, skin care and detoxification. Castor bean seeds were brought to the Americas and cultivated by enslaved people as a medicinal as early as 1687. It's native to Ethiopia.

Castor oil is the only oil that contains ricinoleic acid, an unsaturated omega 9 fatty acid. Rich in glycerides, castor oil is a non-drying oil and emollient. The book of Jonah refers to a plant, "kikayon," which some scholars believe is the castor plant, used by God to provide shade and comfort to Jonah.

When choosing a Castor Oil, always select an organic oil in a dark glass bottle.

Some uses of Castor Oil:

Castor Oil Sleep Mask: at night, cover face and neck with oil on a clean dry face. Avoid eyes. Sleep well and wash in face as usual when rising.

Castor Oil Pack: Traditionally used to detox the body. It is important that pack not be passed from person to person. One pack, one person.

Store your Castor Oil pack in a glass jar between uses.

You will need:
Flannel material.
Organic Castor Oil
A heating pad
A glass jar

Directions:
1. Soak your flannel in the oil.
2. Saturate it but do not have it dripping. It will make a mess and Castor Oil stains can be stubborn.
3. Make sure you lay a towel or sheet down when you are relaxing with a Castor Oil Pack.
4. The pack should be placed in the region of the liver-on the right side of your body, extending from a little bit above the bottom of your sternum (breastbone) to about 4 inches below your navel.
5. The pack should wrap around the body on the right side, from the navel as far to the side as you can get it.
6. You can add a heating pad if that feels comfortable.
7. Keep the pack on for 45 minutes.

Note: Be careful with Castor Oil. Some bodies react with rashes as with everything, ask your medical professional for their thoughts. Asking questions is healing, too!

Part Four: The Healing Lifestyle

Let love of the brothers *and* sisters continue. Do not neglect hospitality to strangers, for by this some have entertained angels without knowing it. Remember the prisoners, as though in prison with them, *and* those who are badly treated, since you yourselves also are in the body

Hebrews 13:1-3

In 1848, Elder Joseph Brackett wrote "Simple Gifts" in his Shaker community in Maine. The Shakers (or United Society of Believers in Christ's Second Appearing) were a small group that left England to find religious tolerance in North America. They believed in simplicity, equality, celibacy, and communal living.

'Tis the gift to be simple, 'tis the gift to be free,
'Tis the gift to come down where we ought to be,
And when we find ourselves in the place just right,
'Twill be in the valley of love and delight.
When true simplicity is gain'd,
To bow and to bend we will not be asham'd,
To turn, turn will be our delight,
Till by turning, turning we come round right.

12 Daily Practices

Now the full number of those who believed were of one heart and soul, and no one said that any of the things that belonged to him was his own, but they had everything in common. And with great power the apostles were giving their testimony to the resurrection of the Lord Jesus, and great grace was upon them all. There was not a needy person among them, for as many as were owners of lands or houses sold them and brought the proceeds of what was sold and laid it at the apostles' feet, and it was distributed to each as any had need.

Acts 4:32-35

The story of Taco Tuesday

In March of 2020, the COVID-19 lockdown restrictions went into place, no church? No WAY! A small but mighty group of scrappy and woodsy Michiganders decided we would meet outside at the home of the Krotzer family. Hope and Rob Krotzer and their brilliant, beautiful children lived on acres and acres of forest in a log cabin Rob built with trees he harvested. A pond stocked with fish cuddles up to the edge of the land where the children swam in the summer and ice skate when winter came. We would build a fire, keep the hot chocolate flowing in the frigid cold, and meet in snowsuits. Home feels like a hug, and it's exactly what we all needed, especially when we were socially distanced. As a newly single person, I needed that hug more than ever. Sure, I am a tree hugger, but these trees and logs, I swear, hug back.

We met every Tuesday for a "come as you are "taco bar and Bible study. We prayed together, cried, and boy, did we eat a lot of tacos. Taco Tuesday started with about 12 people, and it grew into a group large enough to be considered a church where absolutely everyone was welcome. No exceptions. There were dozens of Taco Tuesday salvations and baptisms in the pond. "Pray for the fish," Rob would joke as one recovering addict and radiant child of God named Cloe was immersed on the day of her baptism. When she emerged from the water, white and shining, we saw the face of Jesus. The gospel is not a magic wand. Life on Earth is hard, but oh, so worth living and loving.

When my marriage was failing and I was scared, the Taco Tuesday people supported me and lifted me up in prayer. When it all fell apart, I knew I was not alone. The house I lived in was heated solely with wood. Did I think I could keep the wood chopped and the fire going? No. No, I did not. But the men of Taco Tuesday said, "if your axe gets stuck or your fire goes out, you call us." My axe never got stuck. My fire never went out.

I can do all things through Christ who gives me strength.

Philippians 4:13

How to Host a Clothing Swap

We all have those items in our closets—the "why am I still hanging onto this" items, the "I am never going to wear this again, but it's too good to just donate" items. Enter the Clothing Swap.

The first time I attended one, it was at a girlfriend's house. You can read the story in The Healing Season. Since then, I've attended and hosted so many that at least half of my wardrobe has come from church ladies like me.

Here's what you do:
Invite EVERYONE to come and bring their items:

Ideas:
Dresses, Pants, Skirts, Blouses, Sweaters, Jackets, Shoes, Jewelry, Bags, Skincare, and Perfumes.

- There will be something for everyone.
- Let it up "department store style" and make sure to have plenty of mirrors.
- Snacks and drinks are a great addition.
- By the end of the night, you will not only have cleaned out your closet and filled it with fresh choices, but you will also have laughed and hyped each other up.
- When it's over, you will, like Jesus with his famous loaves and fishes, have baskets of leftovers to share with a shelter or charity shop nearby.

This same model can be used for kids' toys and clothing, tools, appliances. Anything at all. Swap it up, people.

The Miracle of the Loaves and Fishes

This is the only miracle recorded in all four of the Gospels. Rad, huh?!

Matthew 14:13-21

14 When He came ashore, He saw a large crowd, and felt compassion for them and healed their sick.

15 Now when it was evening, the disciples came to Him and said, "This place is secluded and the hour is already past to eat; send the crowds away, so that they may go into the villages and buy food for themselves." 16 But Jesus said to them, "They do not need to go; you give them something to eat!" 17 They *said to Him, "We have nothing here except five loaves and two fish." 18 And He said, "Bring them here to Me." 19 And ordering the crowds to sit down on the grass, He took the five loaves and the two fish, and looked up toward heaven. He blessed the food and breaking the loaves, He gave them to the disciples, and the disciples gave them to the crowds. 20 And they all ate and were satisfied, and they picked up what was left over of the broken pieces: twelve full baskets. 21 There were about five thousand men who ate, besides women and children.

Mark 6:34-44

34 When Jesus went ashore, He saw a large crowd, and He felt compassion for them because they were like sheep without a shepherd; and He began to teach them many things. 35 And when it was already late, His disciples came up to Him and said, "This place is secluded and it is already late; 36 send them away so that they may go into the surrounding countryside and villages and buy themselves something to eat." 37 But He answered them, "You give them something to eat!" And they *said to Him, "Shall we go and spend two hundred denarii on bread, and give it to them to eat?" 38 But He *said to them, "How many loaves do you have? Go look!" And when they found out, they *said, "Five, and two fish." 39 And He ordered them all to recline by groups on the green grass. 40 They reclined in groups of hundreds and fifties. 41 And He took the five loaves and

the two fish, and looking up toward heaven, He blessed the food and broke the loaves and He gave them to the disciples again and again to set before them; and He divided the two fish among them all. 42 And they all ate and were satisfied; 43 and they picked up twelve full baskets of the broken pieces of bread, and of the fish. 44 There were five thousand men who ate the loaves.

Luke 9:12-17

12 Now the day was ending, and the twelve came up and said to Him, "Dismiss the crowd, so that they may go into the surrounding villages and countryside and find lodging and get something to eat; because here, we are in a secluded place." 13 But He said to them, "You give them something to eat!" But they said, "We have no more than five loaves and two fish, unless perhaps we go and buy food for all these people." 14 (For there were about five thousand men.) But He said to His disciples, "Have them recline to eat in groups of about fifty each." 15 They did so, and had them all recline. 16 And He took the five loaves and the two fish, and, looking up to heaven, He blessed them and broke them, and gave them to the disciples again and again, to serve the crowd. 17 And they all ate and were satisfied; and the broken pieces which they had left over were picked up, twelve baskets full.

John 6:4-14

4 Now the Passover, the feast of the Jews, was near. 5 So Jesus, after raising His eyes and seeing that a large crowd was coming to Him, *said to Philip, "Where are we to buy bread so that these people may eat?" 6 But He was saying this only to test him, for He Himself knew what He intended to do. 7 Philip answered Him, "Two hundred denarii worth of bread is not enough for them, for each to receive just a little!" 8 One of His disciples, Andrew, Simon Peter's brother, *said to Him, 9 "There is a boy here who has five barley loaves and two fish; but what are these for so many people?" 10 Jesus said, "Have the people recline to eat." Now there was plenty of grass in the place. So the men reclined, about five thousand in number. 11 Jesus then took the loaves, and after giving thanks He distributed them to those who were reclining; likewise also of the fish, as

much as they wanted. 12 And when they had eaten their fill, He *said to His disciples, "Gather up the leftover pieces so that nothing will be lost." 13 So they gathered them up, and filled twelve baskets with pieces from the five barley loaves which were left over by those who had eaten. 14 Therefore when the people saw the sign which He had performed, they said, "This is truly the Prophet who is to come into the world."

Hack your nervous system with the 5-7-9 Breath

If you need to find some peace in your day, find your breath. This breathing technique helps to release your body from fight-or-flight mode.

Inhale to the count of 5.

Hold your breath to the count of 7.

Exhale to the count of 9.

Now your body knows you are safe.

Repeat as needed.

The Serentiy Prayer

God, Grant me the serenity to accept the things I cannot change,
The courage to change the things I can and,
The wisdom to know the difference.

Adapted

God, Grant me the serenity to accept the people I cannot change,
The courage to change the one I can and,
The wisdom to know that one is me.

13 Hormone Balancing Practices

And God said, "Behold, I have given you every plant yielding seed that is on the face of all the earth, and every tree with seed in its fruit. You shall have them for food.

Genesis 1:29

Menopause & Hot Flashes

Hot flashes are the most common symptom of menopause and perimenopause. Over two-thirds of North American women approaching menopause experience hot flashes. They also affect women who begin menopause following chemotherapy or surgery to remove their ovaries.

Hot flashes occur when blood vessels near the skin's surface dilate to release heat, causing sweating. Some women also experience a rapid heart rate or chills. Conventional medicine suggests no prevention, aside from limiting triggering foods, is available.

There's nothing you can do to avoid hot flashes during menopause, but you can avoid triggers that may make them more frequent or severe. Common triggers include stress, caffeine, alcohol, spicy foods, tight clothing, cigarette smoke, and sugar.

If simple adaptations such as wearing breathable natural fibers and using a cooling pillow do not yield satisfactory results, the doctor is likely to recommend Hormone Replacement Therapy. Side effects of this therapy may include a higher likelihood of blood clots, breast and endometrial cancers, and gallbladder inflammation. Furthermore, when you stop taking HRT, hot flashes may return.

Let's look at some other choices that may help our bodies find ease in this transition.

Considering the events that create this response in the body include changes in reproductive hormones and the body's thermostat (hypothalamus). These changes cause the hypothalamus to become more sensitive to slight changes in body temperature.

Aside from menopause, other possible causes of Hot Flashes include:

Thyroid problems, such as hyperthyroidism, which causes an overabundance of thyroid hormone. This can increase the body's metabolism and lead to hot flashes and sweating. Hypothyroidism is the usual culprit in these cases.

Hormone-secreting tumors, such as pancreatic tumors, override the organs' ability to help the body function properly, leading to hot flashes and sweating. The Mayo Clinic suggests that proper nutrition, including adequate levels of B complex vitamins and vitamin E, can bolster the endocrine system.

Super stars in the "help for hot flash" category can be found in Mother Nature. The best known of these helpers are:

Black Cohosh (Actaea racemosa, Cimicifuga racemosa): This herb has garnered significant scientific attention for its potential effects on hot flashes. Studies evaluating its effectiveness in alleviating hot flashes have yielded mixed results. Nevertheless, some women report that it has been beneficial for them. Recent research indicates that black cohosh does not function like estrogen, contrary to previous beliefs. This alleviates concerns regarding its impact on hormone-sensitive tissues (e.g., uterus, breast). Black cohosh has maintained a strong safety record over the years (menopause.org).

Vitex Agnus Castus: Proven in German studies to assist women with hormonal imbalance issues. Vitex Agnus Castus increases the levels of progesterone in the body. The Vitex Chasteberry Tree contains compounds that affect the pituitary glands. These compounds prompt the pituitary glands to decrease their production of follicle-stimulating hormones (FS) and increase their production of luteinizing hormones (L). This process leads the pituitary gland to produce more progesterone hormones. These hormones are especially important during menopause, and their increase can help women maintain balanced hormone levels. Consequently, Vitex Agnus Castus can be highly effective for menopause, as it supports women in staying hormonally balanced and helps them avoid the unpleasant signs and symptoms of menopause.

Essential Oils: Clary sage, fennel, cypress, angelica, and coriander oils are the go-to choices for supporting hormone balance. The world of essential oils is flooded with excellent and terrible choices. I recommend purchasing your oils from a trusted health store. Oils are powerful and deserve an entirely separate treatment.

Phytoestrogens: Plant-based estrogens. Essential oils that contain phytoestrogens may help balance hormones. Because many of the changes associated with menopause are linked to declining estrogen, phytoestrogens could alleviate a range of symptoms, including mood swings, hot flashes, and irregular periods.

Citrus oil: Aromatherapy is reported to offer several health benefits for women experiencing menopausal symptoms. Researchers in a 2014 study discovered that postmenopausal women who inhaled this essential oil experienced fewer physical symptoms and an increase in sexual desire. Furthermore, they noted a reduction in systolic blood pressure, as well as improvements in pulse rate and estrogen concentrations.

Citrus also has anti-inflammatory properties, which may help with any aches and pains you may be experiencing.

Geranium: Used as an essential oil, it has also been found to help menopausal women manage hormonal changes.

Basil: If you're looking for ways to increase your estrogen levels or improve your mood, consider adding basil aromatherapy to your daily regimen. Diluted basil can also help with hot flashes when applied to your feet or rubbed across the back of your neck.

Rose: Some researchers have proposed that rose oil strengthens the uterus and may help with menstrual cycle issues. During menopause, rose oil could enhance mood and alleviate hot flashes by balancing hormones.

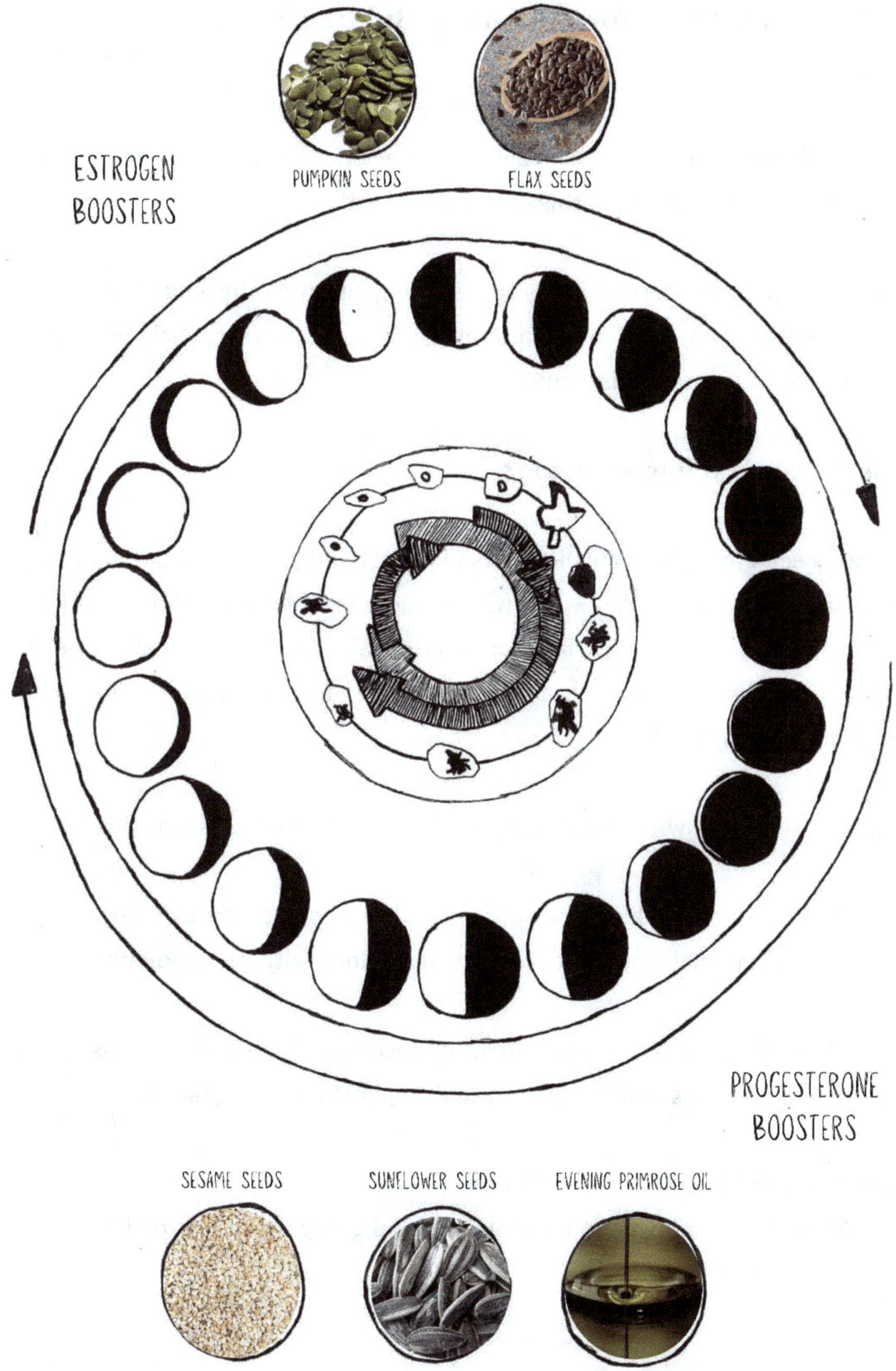

ESTROGEN BOOSTERS — PUMPKIN SEEDS, FLAX SEEDS

PROGESTERONE BOOSTERS — SESAME SEEDS, SUNFLOWER SEEDS, EVENING PRIMROSE OIL

What is Seed Cycling for Hormone Balance?

When I feel my hormones out of balance, this is my first stop.
You can add the seeds to a salad, eat them as a snack or add them to a smoothie.
As always, choose organic and in this case, raw is best.

The basic concept is that certain seeds are estronogenic and others support progesterone. When you eat a small amount of these seed in an intentional way, you support the body as it makes its rounds.

What is the seed cycling schedule?

The average seed cycling schedule involves ingesting one tablespoon of flax (fresh ground seeds or flax meal-not raw and whole) and one tablespoon of pumpkin seeds a day during the first 13 or so days of a menstrual cycle. Then, after ovulation, participants eat one tablespoon of sunflower seeds and one tablespoon of sesame seeds every day until their next period begins.

You can also "double down" on a seed if you choose, but don't cross the phases.

Example: You can have 2 tablespoons of flax seeds a day in the first 13 days.
If you are post menstrual, you can follow this plan along with the moon phases.

New Moon to Full Moon (Days 1-14): Focus on seeds rich in phytoestrogens (plant-based estrogens) like flax and pumpkin, which support the follicular phase.

Full Moon to New Moon (Days 15-28): Shift to seeds that support progesterone production, such as sunflower and sesame seeds, aligning with the luteal phase.

14 Healing Waters

You shall serve the Lord your God, and he will bless your bread and your water, and I will take sickness away from among you.

Exodus 23:25

Blue Solar Water and Ho'Oponopono

There is a tradition in the Hawaiian culture of clearing the air in a family circle by gathering on Sundays for a ritual of love, mercy, and forgiveness, called "Ho'Oponopono."

Translated as "The correction," Ho'Oponopono has a couple of components:

It's Mantra (or repeated phrase)

Thank you.
I love you.
I'm sorry.
Forgive me.

You can either confess and repent in this gathering or offer forgiveness to yourself or someone else. Practitioners also allow these simple statements to replace a negative soundtrack in their minds with uplifting words, thereby firing and wiring new mental circuitry.

Blue Solar Water

Practitioners of Ho'Oponopono often put their drinking water into blue glass bottles and allow the sun to shine on them. Anecdotal evidence suggests that this act purifies the water. When the water is ingested, the mantras accompany it.

Thinking "Thank you" while drinking water from blue glass charged with sunlight.

I once heard a story of a man who served as a psychiatrist in a correctional facility. Of all the inmates, he had the best improvement in his state by far. He says he didn't speak at all during his counseling sessions. Instead, he quietly contemplated the Ho'oponopono mantras, and he credits every improvement to this quiet act.

But whoever drinks of the water that I will give him will never be thirsty again.
The water that I will give him will become in him a spring of water welling up to eternal life.
John 4:14

The Day the Dam Broke

What binds us, sweetens us, and helps us rise? Are the things that break us also the very things that strengthen us?

The Sanford Dam in Michigan failed on May 19, 2020, and washed our little lake town away. We had been in lockdown since March, and when we all retreated to our corners and closed the doors, there was some mumbling and grumbling about the government, the healthcare system, and the goodwill of our neighbors. Even idyllic little Sanford had an air of division, and as scripture states, a house divided against itself cannot stand.

It had been raining for days. The soaking rain makes you question the integrity of your roof. Muck boots splashed with rain poured in sheets for a week or more. "I wonder how that dam is doing" was the topic on everyone's mind. The state was considering it too and took the time to text us a "Don't worry. It's all good." message. And Sanford slept soundly to the patter of an early spring drenching. And then the dam broke.

Choppers overhead. Emergency vehicles with bullhorns driving block by block to evacuate the townspeople. Coming out of a lockdown and into a shelter is, by all measures, hellish. We had our "go kit" in the car. We had a ladder on the side of the house in case the water came fast and we needed to climb to the roof for rescue. We waited. We listened. More text messages came. "Do not evacuate unless you are asked to." They didn't want the streets to become overcrowded. We waited, and the orders, block by block, came right to our corner. They called the people across the street to leave. Our house was the first one that was able to stay. We were spared.

For days, the local fire department worked tirelessly, and linemen from various states arrived to reinstall every electrical pole in town. With the power out, I baked chocolate chip cookies on the grill and passed them out to say, "thank you!"

What happens when you emerge from isolation into a shelter? In Sanford, Michigan, you pull together. Any questions about who flew what flag were washed away in the river's power. We were one. Sanford strong. And so it is to this day. It took years to recover. It's not over yet. Because it was a private dam and not a natural disaster, FEMA was not present. But the churches from all over the country flooded in when the water receded. As Mr. Rogers is famously credited with saying, "Look for the helpers." They are everywhere. One woman created a Heart of Sanford memorial where townspeople could write or draw their memories and prayers. A retired counselor started a free community grief group. Musicians began a festival on the anniversary of the break called the Dam Bash. Everyone comes out. Everyone is welcome just as they are.

Water Therapy

Up to 60% of the human adult body consists of water. The brain and heart are made up of 73% water, while the lungs contain about 83% water. The skin is composed of 64% water, muscles and kidneys comprise 79%, and even the bones are made up of a watery 31%.

Water is a big deal not just in the natural world but also in the supernatural. In Christianity, we see the scary tradition of baptism. We see the healing pools of the Bible, and the Bible even tells us that God collects the waters. Jesus says he will give us streams of Living Water.

He could have used any symbol. He chose water.

If you've ever investigated Dr. Emoto's research on the effects of words on water, you have seen the impact of words on water. If one speaks kind words over water, and under the microscope, we see droplets organized into lacy, snowflake-like shapes. When exposed to negative words, the water becomes scattered and splattered. Since we are made of water, it follows that we should be wise about what we allow to be spoken over and around us.

We are facing a water emergency on Earth, yet many of us (myself included) have access to clean water. This book aims to help us make the most of it.

Do you have a special water source? Maybe it's a particular stretch of ocean or a vast lake. Maybe it's the pond behind a cabin in the woods. We all have our sacred waters.

As a kid, I lived in the woods on Michigan's Upper Peninsula. Near my home, there was a spring called Norway Spring. I'd run there in the morning before school to drink the ice-cold, slippery-fresh water. To this day, it's the best water I had ever tasted. It was the minerals the grandmas said. As always, Grandma was right.

The world's oldest medical literature makes numerous references to the beneficial use of the bath in treating various diseases. The learned Greek Hippocrates, who lived about five hundred years before Christ and is referred to as the "father of modern medicine," was the first to write extensively on the healing of diseases with water. He used water extensively, both internally and externally, to treat illnesses of all kinds.

Bathing was prominent in the instructions Moses, under divine guidance, gave for the government of the Hebrew nation. The relationship of bathing to the treatment of leprosy would lead us to believe that it was used for its curative effects.

The ancient Persians and Greeks began to build public bathing facilities, erecting stately and magnificent buildings dedicated to bathing. The first bathhouse in Rome was constructed around 33 B.C.E., and the city of Bath, England, is named for the enormous Roman bath that remains there to this day. If you visit Bath (which I've had the blessing to do), you can immerse yourself in the healing waters at the Therma Spa. I can say that when I went, I had a significant bruise on my leg that healed rapidly after the waters. I'm a believer.

But the water is healing water, not magic water. So, why?

Why did soldiers return home from war to the waters? What's the deal? Well...God, of course. He provided us with the water. How can we enjoy its benefits without traveling to Bath, England, and instead, perhaps enjoy a similar experience in our own bathrooms?

Good question! First, let's look at this water's composition:

All thermal waters contain high concentrations of sodium, calcium, chloride, and sulfate ions. Hot springs can be found all over this planet. From India to Antarctica, hot and cold places alike are abundant with healing waters.

Geronimo is said to have spent an entire year in Hot Springs, New Mexico, healing in waters that you can visit today.

That spring, by the way, is composed of chloride, sodium, bicarbonate, calcium, sulfate, potassium, silicate, silicon, and magnesium

What happens to the human body in water? What physiological changes occur when your body is immersed in warm water? What happens to the circulatory, pulmonary, and musculoskeletal systems?

For starters:

1. Cardiac output increases by 32% (at rest) during neck immersion.
2. The total work of breathing increases by 60%, and expiratory reserve volumes decrease by 75% during neck immersion.
3. Muscle blood flow increases by 225% (at rest) during neck immersion.

Famous Healing Hot Springs

Why is it called a Bathtub? The answer is that Bath England's healing water and the Roman Hot Spring Healing Center it created changed the way the world heals.

A study published in the journal *Microbe* has uncovered a diverse array of microorganisms in the geothermal waters of the Roman Baths that may possess super-healing properties.

Bath, known as Aquae Sulis during the Roman period, is located in the modern city of Bath, England. The Romans built a bathing complex and temple at the site of three natural hot springs, which are heated by geothermal activity, raising the water temperature to between 40 and 45°C.

In a recent study by the University of Plymouth, scientists collected samples of water, sediment, and biofilm from the King's Spring and the Great Bath. The samples were then analyzed using metagenomic sequencing to explore the bacterial and archaeal communities. The sequencing revealed 300 distinct types of bacteria, including Actinobacteria and Myxococcota, which are known for producing antibiotics.

Further tests revealed that 15 of these isolates – including examples of Proteobacteria and Firmicutes – exhibited varying levels of inhibition against human pathogens, such as E. coli, Staphylococcus aureus, and Shigella flexneri. According to the study authors: "From this data, there is clear potential for novel antimicrobial natural products from the Roman Baths, as demonstrated by other thermal hot springs globally."

The Hot Springs in Truth or Consequences, NM

For hundreds of years, Native Americans met at the hot mineral springs that flowed from the ground where the town of Truth or Consequences (formerly Hot Springs, NM) is now located. They bathed, socialized, and cared for their wounds and ailments, discovering that the waters had inherent healing properties. It is believed that the famous Apache warrior Geronimo soaked in these springs. In the late 16th century, the Spanish arrived, and eventually, white settlers began moving into the ranch and mine. Today, the area is widely called the most affordable hot springs in the United States.

MINERAL CONTENT of the GEOTHERMAL SPRINGS in TRUTH OR CONSEQUENCES, NEW MEXICO

ANALYSIS DETERMINED BY THE LOS ALAMOS NATIONAL LABORATORY AT LOS ALAMOS, NEW MEXICO FROM SAMPLES TAKEN MAY 31, 1987

ELEMENT		PPM	ELEMENT		PPM
Ag	Silver	.001	Li	Lithium	1.20
Al	Aluminum	.05	Mg	Magnesium	15.30
As	Arsenic	.05	Mo	Molybdenum	0.002
Au	Gold	0.005	Na	Sodium	751.0
B	Boron	0.25	NH4	Ammonium	0.05
Ba	Barium	0.20	Ni	Nickel	0.002
Br	Bromine	2.60	NO3	Nitrate	0.20
Ca	Calcium	163.0	Pb	Lead	0.002
Cd	Cadmium	0.001	PO4	Phosphate	0.20

Cl	Chloride	1360.0	Rb	Ribidium	0.70
Co	Cobalt	0.002	Sb	Antimony	0.05
Cr	Cromium	0.002	Se	Selenium	0.05
Cs	Cesium	0.12	Si	Silicon	21.0
Cu	Copper	0.002	SiO2	Silicate	45.0
F	Fluoride	3.02	SO4	Sulfate	75.10
Fe	Iron	0.02	Sr	Strontium	3.82
HCO3	Bicarbonate	220.0	U	Uranium	0.10
Hg	Mercury	0.05	Zn	Zinc	0.01
K	Potassium	56.0			

Source: Riverbend Hot Springs, *MINERAL CONTENT of the GEOTHERMAL SPRINGS in TRUTH OR CONSEQUENCES, NEW MEXICO*, Los Alamos National Laboratory, May 1987.

Epsom Salt

Epsom salt, also known as magnesium sulfate, is a naturally occurring compound containing magnesium, sulfur, and oxygen. Its crystalline structure is similar to that of common table salt or sodium chloride.

The miraculous qualities of the mineral spring on Epsom Common were discovered in 1618. The story is that in a dry summer, Henry Wicker found a source of water on Epsom Common, which his cattle refused to drink. This water proved to have medicinal properties, first used externally to cure sores but later found to be a purgative when drunk. So, Epsom rapidly became a prosperous health resort—a spa.

To create a home spa with Epsom Salt, draw a warm bath and add two cups of Epsom Salt. Allow the salt to dissolve completely, then relax in the water for at least 20 minutes to absorb the minerals.

Add optional oils like lavender, jasmine, or geranium.

Dead Sea Salt

For this therapy, you can find salt at the nearest store (every Dollar Tree I've been to carries it) and follow its directions or add 2 cups to a tub! It's recommended to soak for at least 20 minutes to absorb the minerals and then rinse your body with cold water.

Compress & Immersion in Water as Therapy.

It gives us relief from the gravity of the earth and the heaviness of life. After our class, my teacher gives each sweaty participant an ice-cold washcloth. I promise it's highly therapeutic.

So, what feels best to you? What would you like to explore?

Perhaps you choose to place a cold towel on the back of your neck in the heat. Perhaps you submerge your feet in hot water while applying a cold towel to your face, head, or neck. Perhaps you offer a cold towel to someone on the street. Perhaps you immerse yourself in salt from the Dead Sea (available cheaply on Amazon). Perhaps you soak in the minerals of an Epsom bath. Perhaps you take a trip to a body of water, whether near or far. Or perhaps you set your lawn chair in the baby pool with the kids or run carefree in a splash park.

Whatever you choose: Water. Is. Healing.

Wise Water Tea – Traditional Ayurvedic

Tea drinking is also considered water therapy. This combination of three herbs increases digestive ability and is extremely effective as a delicious detoxification tonic.

Best of all, it's EASY!

You will need:
Water
1 teaspoon cumin
1 teaspoon coriander
1 teaspoon fennel

Directions:
1. Boil 1 liter of water.
2. Place in a non-plastic thermos or 1-liter canning jar with a lid.
3. Add 1 teaspoon cumin, coriander, and fennel.
4. Let steep for about 15 minutes.
5. Strain the solids.

Drink a cup before breakfast and sip the rest throughout the day.

This was introduced to me by my first Ayurveda teacher. Tracey emphasized the importance of selecting organic herbs. She carried tea with her everywhere. This tea helped restore my digestion after having my son. Thank you, Tracey!

15 Bedtime Practices and Prayers

He lets me lie down in green pastures;
He leads me beside quiet waters.
He restores my soul;
He guides me in the paths of righteousness
For the sake of His name.

Psalm 23:2-3

Preparing Yourself

Chamomile tea, warm oat milk with honey, and a few cashews. What do they have in common? They all soothe your nervous system. Nighttime is the right time for these treats. It's also the right time for a dark, screen-free room.

Get ready for bed. Clean and moisturize your skin, and brush your teeth. Allow your workday to slip away and reduce the high-speed train of your thoughts. This is a time to limit or eliminate screens and lights of all kinds. Avoid watching or reading stressful and violent content before sleep. This mental space as you drift off is the best place to envision your most wonderful life. Carry it into your dreams. If there was an unfortunate interaction from that day, you can reshape it in your mind at this moment.

Then, leave it with God.

Restorative Yoga for Sleep – Legs Up the Wall

Does this sound familiar? You (or a family member) need sleep but just…can't. Your mind is racing, and the clock keeps ticking forward. Don't despair! You have a helper built right into your nervous system.

When you place your feet above your heart and head, it communicates to your body that you are safe. You send a signal to your brain that you don't need to run, allowing the energy (and blood) to flow out of your legs and rest in your heart and head, which enables your systems to relax and drop you into sweet relaxation.

Here's what to do:

If your bed is against a wall, you can do this in bed. Otherwise, you can perform this exercise against a wall while lying on the floor.

Getting in:

First, sit your left hip and left shoulder flush to the wall with your legs extended.

As you exhale, swing your legs up the wall until both of your glutes are evenly positioned against the wall and your back comfortably rests on the floor or bed. When you look up, your feet should be aligned, and your knees should be relaxed.

Rest with your arms and hands at your sides, or place one hand on your belly and one hand on your heart. Do this for at least 3-5 minutes.

Coming out:

First, bend your knees and place the soles of your feet against the wall. Pause for a deep breath. Roll onto your right side and rest for a moment. When you feel ready, either drift off to sleep or press yourself up using the strength of your hands and arms. Pause before standing if you are getting up from this position, or simply enjoy a sweet rest.

This yoga pose was my daughter's favorite when she was little. Her body naturally wanted to enter this restful position. You may find that, like my daughter, placing your legs up the wall is the best way to destress and regulate an anxious mind.

Bedtime Prayers

Captured like spun sugar in the nostalgia of my youth is a television show called The Waltons. It aired on Sunday nights throughout the 70s and into the 80s. The story of a farming family, poor in money but rich in love, was exactly what we all needed: the beauty of simplicity, the connective tissue of shared ups and downs - family and love.

Each night, the family retired to bed at the same time, and the show iconically ended with an evening exterior shot of their humble home as they each said "Goodnight" to one another by name. If you've ever heard the phrase "Goodnight, John boy" and wondered about its origin, now you know.

The practice of blessing your family at bedtime is probably as old as the concepts of family and bedtime. Here is a lovely Jesuit family prayer:

"Thank you God, for this day,

Thank you for our family.

We're sorry for the things we did that didn't make you happy.

Help us to be better people, help us love each other.

Help us honor you, our Father.

Bless the people of the world.

Bless our loved ones, far and near.

Finally, we lift up to You

This request for You to hear:

(Insert any special intention)

We love You, Lord."

Perhaps the earliest recorded version of a bedtime prayer was written by George Wheeler in his 1698 book *The Protestant Monastery*, which reads:

"Upon lying down and going to sleep.

Here I lay me down to sleep.

To thee, O Lord, I give my Soul to keep,

Wake I ever, Or Wake I never;

To thee O Lord, I give my Soul to keep forever."

A later version printed in *The New England Primer* goes:

"Now I lay me down to sleep,

I pray the Lord my Soul to keep [;]

If I should die before I 'wake,

I pray the Lord my Soul to take."

Other versions

Grace Bridges, 1932:

"Now I lay me down to sleep,

I pray my lord my soul to keep,

In the morn when I awake

Please teach me the path of life to take.

Now I lay me down to sleep,

I pray the Lord my soul to keep;

His Love to guard me through the night,

And wake me in the morning's light amen.

Now I lay me down to sleep,

I pray the Lord my soul to keep;

Please angels watch me through the night,

And keep me safe till morning light.

Now I lay me down to sleep,

I pray the Lord my soul to keep;

Angels watch me through the night,

And wake me with the morning light.

Amen

Now I wake to see the light,

As God has kept me through the night;

And now I lift my voice to pray,

That Thou wilt keep me through the day.

Now I lay me down to sleep,

I pray the Lord my soul to keep,

See me safely through the night,

And wake me with the morning light. Amen.

The version we said at bedtime in my family

Now I lay me down to sleep,

I pray the Lord my soul to keep,

When in the morning light I wake,

Show me the path of love to take.

Amen."

My family would follow this prayer up with a never-ending list of "God blesses," such as:

"God bless mom and dad.

God bless Grandma Mary and Grandma Nora. God bless Grandma Kathy and Grandma Kay. God bless Aunty Mickey and my uncles.

God bless all people, everywhere.

May the be happy, peaceful and safe.

May all have enough food and water and love.

Thank you that even when we are far away, you hold us together.

In Jesus name,

Amen."

God, You provide. You send friends and peace and sun and rain and food to the fields.

You've seen use through before.

You'll see us through together today.

God, give us what we need.

You stood with our ancestors in hard times and they came away with wonderful recipes to pass on with their stories.

May we do the same today.

Sweeten us with your joy, bind us in unity and help us rise in hope.

With hearts and bellies full we give you glory.

Show us how to work as a body.

Made different but with one purpose.

Love.

In Jesus name,

Amen.

References

Francis, Raymond. Never Fear CANCER Again. Health Communications INC., 2011.

Gerson, Charlotte, and Morton Walker. The Gerson Therapy. Kensington Books, 2001.

Hobbs, Christopher, and Kathi Keville. Women's Herbs Women's Health. Botanica Press, 2007.

Hoffman, David. Medical Herbalism. Healing Arts Press, 2003.

Lad, Vasant. Ayurveda: The Science of Self-Healing. Lotus Press, 1984.

Nakazawa, Donna Jackson. The Autoimmune Epidemic. Touchstone, 2008.

Stengler, Mark. The Natural Physician's Healing Therapies. Prentice Hall Press, 2001.

Thiel, Robert J. Naturopathy for the 21st Century. Whitman Publications, 2017.

Special thanks to,

7SOUND & CO CREATIVE AGENCY
An Innovative Collaborative Network
7SOUND.CO

One Egg Noodles
Recipes that Hold Us Together

NAME:

INGREDIENTS:

DIRECTIONS:

One Egg Noodles
Recipes that Hold Us Together

NAME:

INGREDIENTS:

DIRECTIONS:

One Egg Noodles
Recipes that Hold Us Together

NAME:

INGREDIENTS:

DIRECTIONS:

One Egg Noodles
Recipes that Hold Us Together

NAME:

INGREDIENTS:

DIRECTIONS:

One Egg Noodles
Recipes that Hold Us Together

NAME:

INGREDIENTS:

DIRECTIONS:

One Egg Noodles
Recipes that Hold Us Together

NAME:

INGREDIENTS:

DIRECTIONS:

One Egg Noodles
Recipes that Hold Us Together

NAME:

INGREDIENTS:

DIRECTIONS:

One Egg Noodles
Recipes that Hold Us Together

NAME:

INGREDIENTS:

DIRECTIONS:

About the Author

Shannyn Cook Caldwell is a National Christian Radio Host, a mom of two grown children and a devoted follower of Jesus.

Her other books include The Healing Season: How a Deadly Tornado Wrecked and Reshaped My Faith, The 40-Day Healing Season and Raised Catholic.

She is a Certified Holistic Nutritionist, a Traditional Naturopathic Doctor (Gensis School of Natural Health) and a Registered Yoga Teacher (Yahweh Yoga).

When she's not talking about God or in the kitchen, she can be found hiking New Mexico with her dogs Bob and Dylan.

www.ingramcontent.com/pod-product-compliance
Lightning Source LLC
Chambersburg PA
CBHW080412170426
43194CB00015B/2787